All Things New

ALL THINGS NEW

BREAKING THE CYCLE AND RAISING A JOYFUL FAMILY

ERIN McCOLE CUPP

Our Sunday Visitor
Huntington, Indiana

Nihil Obstat
Msgr. Michael Heintz, Ph.D.
Censor Librorum

Imprimatur
✠ Kevin C. Rhoades
Bishop of Fort Wayne-South Bend
December 19, 2020

The Nihil Obstat and Imprimatur are official declarations that a book is free from doctrinal or moral error. It is not implied that those who have granted the Nihil Obstat and Imprimatur agree with the contents, opinions, or statements expressed.

Except where noted, Scripture texts in this work are taken from the New American Bible, Revised Edition © 2010, 1991, 1986, 1970 Confraternity of Christian Doctrine, Washington, D.C., and are used by permission of the copyright owner. All rights reserved. No part of the New American Bible may be reproduced in any form without permission in writing from the copyright owner.

Every reasonable effort has been made to determine copyright holders of excerpted materials and to secure permissions as needed. If any copyrighted materials have been inadvertently used in this work without proper credit being given in one form or another, please notify Our Sunday Visitor in writing so that future printings of this work may be corrected accordingly.

The ideas expressed here and elsewhere in the author's work are those of the author alone and do not represent the endorsement or position of the Lay Fraternities of Saint Dominic or the Order of Preachers as a whole.

Our Sunday Visitor Publishing Division, Our Sunday Visitor, Inc., 200 Noll Plaza, Huntington, IN 46750; 1-800-348-2440; www.osv.com

ISBN: 978-1-68192-421-2 (Inventory No. T2314)
1. FAMILY & RELATIONSHIPS—Parenting—General
2. RELIGION—Christian Life—Family
3. RELIGION—Christianity—Catholic

eISBN: 978-1-68192-422-9
LCCN: 2020942141

Cover/interior design: Chelsea Alt
Cover art: Adobe Stock

Printed in the United States of America

To my children,

who will gleefully tell you how often
I fail to take my own advice.

Thank you for pointing me to heaven in all you do.

TABLE OF CONTENTS

Introduction — An Empty Jug 9

1. You Shall Love the Lord, Your God 21

2. You Shall Love Your Neighbor as Yourself 41

3. Blessed Are the Poor in Spirit 73

4. Blessed Are They Who Mourn 95

5. Blessed Are the Meek 115

6. Blessed Are They Who Hunger and
   Thirst for Righteousness 133

7. Blessed Are the Merciful 151

8. Blessed Are the Clean of Heart 175

9. Blessed Are the Peacemakers 191

10. Blessed Are They Who Are Persecuted
    for the Sake of Righteousness 211

Conclusion 231

Resources 241

Bibliography 245

Acknowledgments 249

AN EMPTY JUG

The jar of flour did not go empty, nor the
jug of oil run dry, according to the word
of the LORD spoken through Elijah.
— 1 Kings 17:16

Tunnels Through Ash, Flowers on Stone
On May 18, 1980, in Washington State, the volcano Mount Saint Helens erupted. An entire slope of the once-conical mountain collapsed in a dramatic landslide of super-heated gas and rock. The devastation that followed killed every living thing, including fifty-seven humans, in two hundred square miles. The rich pine forest that covered the acreage around the mountain was simply sheared off, clogging nearby bodies of water with thousands upon thousands of naked, heat-blasted logs. The mountain's pyroclastic flow didn't just singe the earth. It scorched everything

in its path, plunging into neighboring Spirit Lake and boiling away every sign of life in its waters.[1]

As soon as it was deemed safe, the United States Geological Survey sent scientists to what became called the "blowdown zone" or "blast zone." The USGS didn't just send geologists, however. They also sent biologists, looking for signs of life in the devastation. With that level of destruction, nobody expected to see anything but barren dust for at least a decade, probably more. The eruption had blanketed the soil with nutrient-poor ash, hostile to most plants. The pyroclastic flow had cooked the lake's inhabitants and deprived the waters of oxygen, making it inhospitable at best to any wandering species looking for a new settling spot.

Then, something unexpected happened. Not three months after the explosion, there were signs of tunneling through the ash — the types of tunnels made by the northern pocket gopher, a species protected from the volcano's effects by its burrowing habits. Less than a year after the eruption, biologists were even further surprised to find an actual plant in full flower in the most devastated, least fertile area of the blast zone. This flower, a purple-and-white-bloomed prairie lupine, managed to establish itself in the layers of barren ash thanks to its root structure, which hosts bacteria, which in turn provide the host lupine's roots with the nitrogen that volcanic ash lacks.

As first months then years went by, USGS scientists were ever more shocked by how quickly species after species returned to the region, bringing color and life back to the blast zone. A process that wasn't expected to start for at least ten years began in only three months. While the area around Mount Saint Helens will always show evidence of the May 18, 1980, eruption, it also shows abundant proof that nature's default state in the face of devastation is rebirth.

---

1. *Mount Saint Helens: Back From the Dead.* Directed by Nick Davidson (Boston: WGBH, 2010), DVD.

Different Coast, Different Blast Zone
I resist thinking about what I may have been doing on May 18, 1980. I would have been six years old, living on the coast opposite Mount Saint Helens. May 18th was a Sunday that year, so we probably went to Mass some time that morning. That much I can guess with reasonable confidence. What happened that day besides? I don't really want to wonder. Perhaps nothing happened of either monumental goodness or badness, but I automatically resist thinking about any part of my childhood. Why? Isn't childhood supposed to be a joyful romp? Isn't childhood designed to be spent learning the art of unconditional love at the feet of able mentors? Isn't the soil of childhood supposed to be rich and encouraging, full of emotional nutrients that make fussy babies flower into mature, caring, empathetic adults?

It's supposed to be all those things, yes. But for some of us, it's just a barren blanket of blasted ash.

I don't need to go into much detail to express that the way I was parented left me with few positive memories of growing up. I don't need many words to convince you that looking back at my own parents' methods of dealing with me as a child did nothing but teach me how I *don't* want to parent. I only need the shadow of language to express that my childhood was a time of helplessness, of not mattering, of screaming to have my pain heard only to be told to stop screaming so much or the neighbors will hear, don't you know this neighborhood is some kind of echo chamber? People are trying to sleep, you know.

If you've picked up this book, you probably don't need too many details from me. You can fill in your own from your own life. You, too, know what it feels like to hurt the most at the hands of the people God meant to love you the most. You know what it means to not matter when you should, to be called selfish for asking to matter, to never know enough, do enough, or be enough to the people who are supposed to love you unconditionally, who shouldn't *ask* you to be enough of *anything.*

If you've picked up this book, you probably look back at your childhood and see devastation, barrenness, nothing to call nurturing. Nothing to call sacrificial love. Nothing vibrant enough to call "life." I'll bet that you, too, also feel the same dread when well-meaning people chuckle phrases like, "Like mother, like daughter!" or, "A chip off the old block!" or, "The apple doesn't fall far from the tree!" Like me, you look at your childhood and know how you *don't* want to raise your own children, but you also have received precious little training in how you *do* want to parent.

The good news is that, if you've picked up this book, you are interested in breaking this cycle. What happened to previous generations of children in your family will not happen in yours, not if you can help it. Chances are that, like me, you've done some reading on the types of wounds carried by adults whose childhoods were less than ideal. Maybe you've joined support groups, sought therapy, journaled, and ruminated over what you survived, but all that reading and thinking and working focused on the past. What about your future, especially raising your future — your children?

Wanting the buck to stop with you, you picked up countless parenting books, articles, blogs, podcasts, searching for a list of things to do, for positives, for words to come out of your mouth that are healing and not rehashes of hurtful slurs once thrown your small and vulnerable way. You grew your parenting to-do list, but those articles never said anything about what it feels like to give something you yourself never received. They didn't explain how it feels to give actual, self-donative love to both our own parents and our own children, and not receive it back from either direction just yet, because you are flanked by, frankly, emotional children. On the one side, you have your own children, appropriately immature. On the other side, you have your own parents who should have grown up by now.

There's a gap between healing the past and having a future

worth looking forward to. You're reading this book because you want, with God's help, to create a bridge across that gap here in the parenting present.

The Most Healing Thing

When I was pregnant with my oldest kids (that's not a mistake: I have twins), I was anxiously exploring the reality of having to take care of not one but two completely dependent humans, desperately preparing to treat them better than I myself had been treated. To that end, I thought I'd join an online support group for women who'd experienced one type of abuse I had experienced as a child. We were the walking wounded, sometimes bandaging each other's wounds, sometimes too broken ourselves to do much more than hear another's cries. It was hard.

Whenever the topic of having children came up in this group, the one thing I remember reading from others most often was some variation on, "I'm never having kids. I'm too messed up. I don't want to repeat the cycle." Pregnant as I was (and pro-life to boot), I began to doubt the wisdom of even having children. After all, I was no better than the other women in the support group. Who did I think I was, imagining that I of all people could be a good parent when so many who hadn't been parented well went on to abuse their kids? And if my parents, as they'd told me, had treated me that way because it was the best they could do, they couldn't help themselves, and I deserved it, then wasn't I just doomed to be like them?

Then my children were born, and I was amazed. I realize that not everyone is called to parenthood, but in taking care of my own children, I saw that how I had been treated at that same age was, quite simply, wrong. Things I had been told were my fault were not at all my fault. The parent who "couldn't help herself" was exposed as having made the choice to care more about herself than about the helpless, vulnerable child I had been. I learned that parenting was the most healing thing I could have done, and it was through the very responsibility of raising my children that I found God's protection for both my children and myself. Needing to protect them is what empowered me to cut off contact with my abusive mother. Accepting God's gift of children put my healing into motion.

That's not to say I considered myself fully equipped to handle the challenges of parenting. Okay, technically, nobody is equipped outside of God's grace to raise another human being. We're all going to sin against each other, including parents sinning against their own children. That said, I still struggle with times of darkness in my parenting walk. I dig so deep to give my children the kindness I know they deserve as children of God, but they are fallen children of God, and they are prone to disobedience just like the rest of us. For years I just thought I was a "yeller," until I realized I was reacting to the echoes of pain left over from my own childhood. Having my children not listen to me felt distinctly similar to having my parents not care about me. Having to answer my children's natural demands scratched at the wounds left by the unreasonable demands my parents had placed on me.

I've often said that I was the only adult in my family of origin. I'm not going to lie: It hurts to always feel like the only adult around. It hurts to stand firm in the deepest throes of parenting struggles when one did not receive that same mercy in one's own childhood. It hurts to provide something we never received.

In the end, as much as I knew what *not* to do, I still was searching for what *to* do.

The Parenting Pantry

Let's go back to May 1980. I was mostly eating out of boxes. See, we Generation X kids were raised by the first generation to eat prepackaged foods. By that time, it was expected that bread came in a bag, macaroni and cheese came from a box, cake came from a mix, and soup came from a can. I don't know what you heard in your house growing up, but making a cake from scratch was too hard, spaghetti sauce took too long, and bread was too hard *and* took too long. That's not to say we never had those things from scratch (well, I don't think I ever had cake from scratch until I was an adult), but if we did get them, they tasted weird to my lazy palate, and they were seasoned liberally with, "Look at all this hard work I did for you! You'd better appreciate it!"

I give you this metaphor not to shame any of us for using prepackaged foods (seriously, were I to shame anybody for convenience foods I'd be a screaming hypocrite with a jar of red sauce on her counter). I'm using this parallel so that you can imagine with me.

Imagine you need to make dinner for your family. You open up your pantry, looking for ingredients. What do you find? This box is expired. That can is bulging and oozing something green. This bag is full of some kind of pasta-eating beetle. That jar has ants crawling up the threads like tiny mountaineers. There's nothing to eat except rock-bottom basics: some flour, a little bit of oil, some salt. Whatever you make, it'll have to be from absolute scratch.

Looking at parenting after an unsafe childhood can feel a lot like the above scenario. Adults whose parents were decent role models have people to look up to and examples to follow. They have inherited parenting habits that tend to help, not hurt. Those adults arrived at parenthood with a pre-stocked pantry, and they're ready to whip up some fast-and-easy chow. Some of us — those of us reading this book, most likely — are not so lucky.

Not lucky? Okay, fine. But blessed? Absolutely. Blessed how? Blessed with enough parenting pantry basics to craft a joyful family life.

What to Expect from This Book
No, I wasn't able to jump into parenting with a bunch of quick-and-ready parenting tools to make my life and my kids' lives

easier. Chances are, if you're reading this book, you can relate. We're survivors, you and I. That's the good news. The even better news is that, by God's generosity, we can look at the present and future with abundant joy that, in turn, can build a hopeful future for our children and bring healing not just to our own past but even to the people who caused our wounds. This is the healing that transcends the boundaries of past, present, and future. That healing may not look the way you want it to. I can pretty much guarantee it won't look the way your abusers want it to. It's the kind of healing that says, "Yes, I died at your hands, but God makes all things new: even you."

This is exactly the kind of healing that Jesus came to give us, *all* of us: us, our children, and even our abusers.

It is my hope that, by reading this book, you will pick up simple, quality ingredients for what I like to call your "parenting pantry." Each chapter will provide lessons on how different scriptural principles bring peace and holiness to family relationships, both present and past. We'll take a look at the painful memories and habits that, were we to adopt them, would only perpetuate those cycles we are striving to escape. After facing the negatives with open eyes, however, we will also look at the positives: The simple things you can do differently to bring joy rather than pain or indifference into your family life, today and for the future. We'll do this chapter-by-chapter, looking at how the two greatest commandments and the eight Beatitudes provide us straightforward ingredients, or "Beatitude Basics," for healthy parent-child relationships. We'll then create a "Beatitude Basic Workshop," which will provide some options on ways we can consider, pray, live, and model these Beatitude Basics with our families of origin, our children, and ourselves.

Each chapter will offer a "Holy Family Moment," where we'll study how each of these principles was lived out by the Holy Family. You'll also find "Saint-spiration," brief illustrations of how heroes of our faith who were wounded by those who were supposed to love them, through their attachment to our heavenly Father gave these saints the freedom to love even the people who had hurt them most. Finally, each chapter will close with prayers from all ages of our faith tradition that address wounds often felt most keenly by survivors of family abuse and dysfunction.

By offering these tools, this book will show you how to take a hand with God in shaping your future, in what type of parent you become, while keeping a thoughtful eye on the past. Leaving destructive cycles behind to create a family life of joy is uncharted territory for all of us. I invite you to think of this book as less of an end-all, be-all how-to and as more of a guidebook. It's a guide in the same way a tour book provides information about an unfamiliar place but still leaves you room to make your own discoveries. A tour guide can point out things you haven't yet found, but that doesn't mean the guide knows everything there is to know, and that guide is, in many ways, taking the same tour you are, learning along with you.

Finally, this is a book about building a family life that will never be perfect but can certainly be full of joy. A joyful family life might not necessarily even be very good, and it's not guaranteed to produce "great kids." Kids are what they make of themselves with the gifts God has given them. In other words, they're just like you and me. *Joy* is the focus of relationships in this book because joy is the fruit of peace. Peace comes from acceptance of the truth. Acceptance is the fruit of repentance of those times we did wrong and the forgiveness we can grow into, to offer God's mercy to others who did us wrong in their own emotional immaturity.

Here is also the place where I step humbly before you and admit that I'm not the perfect tour guide. I have no advanced degree in psychology, neurology, child development — I was a theatre major, for heaven's sake. My experience with therapy has been spent on the couch, not at the desk. I've learned a lot, but I'm not the best example of how to parent with joy and connection after having been raised with abuse and neglect. I am still wounded. I still respond from those wounds. I have in turn wounded my children. In trying to correct all of my parents' mistakes, I have been quite blind to many of my own. I look at myself writing this book and I feel horribly inadequate. I feel like a fraud.

And I thank God for that.

I thank God for that because my many failures remind me that I don't want you listening to me anyway. I want us both, fellow cycle-breaker, to listen to God. I come before you just as Saint Paul came before the Corinthians. He wrote in his first letter to them that he did not come with great words, impressive smarts, or clever persuasion. No, he came offering nothing of his own power. He came offering the power of God, crucified and risen from the dead. Paul didn't want anyone listening to him in his weakness. He wanted everyone to listen to God, the perfect Father: perfectly strong, perfectly united with the Son and the Spirit, giving us the perfect family that will never use, abuse, neglect, or destroy.

The only perfect family is the Holy Trinity, and that job's taken. The Trinity's job is not to make us perfect parents but to enfold us, our children, and even our parents in their all-perfect love. My prayer for you is the same as Paul's for the Colossians: that we will be filled with spiritual wisdom and understanding that helps us not just to be worthy of parenthood but worthy of the Lord, which will strengthen us "with every power, in accord with his glorious might, for all endurance and patience, with joy" (Col 1:9–11).

This is not a discipline book. This is a love book.

Why Bring God into It Anyway?

Can't we just rely on secular psychology to give us the answers to all our parenting questions? Certainly psychology provides a great deal of insight, tools, and options on how to raise a happy family, but there does tend to be a dimension missing from the purely secular takes. Secular psychology's goal is to help us be happy in the here and now, but "here and now" only lasts so long. Our faith shows us how to be happy and holy forever and how to lead others into that same eternal joy. The secular analysis has great value, but it does not have the only value or the only answers. Sometimes it doesn't even have all the questions.

God, however, has it all and wants to share it all with us. Take a look at 1 Kings 17:10–16. In this passage, the prophet Elijah travels to the house of a widow. There has been an unrelenting drought throughout the land. Everyone is hungry. Elijah asks the widow to take care of him, but she admits that she was about to cook the last of her food, all she had for her son and herself. After that, there would be nothing, and they would starve to death. Elijah asks the widow to bring him some of that food anyway. For some reason, the widow trusts. She feeds Elijah out of what little she has, and instead of dying after this final meal, their flour and oil multiply until the drought breaks. This little, broken family survives.

This is just one of the many examples God gives us of what happens when we trust him with what little we have. This takes on special meaning for survivors of family abuse when we admit that what our past has given us is unusable or, as my friend Mandy[*2] calls it, "Starting from zero." This takes on further meaning when we realize that, in this fallen world, the only thing God did not give us is sin — neither our own nor the sins of those who have made us and our children suffer. What God does give us and has always given us is a way to him, to his perfect fatherly heart that always nurtures even in the face of betrayal.

He gives us the Holy Trinity, showing us that pure, selfless relationship begets new life. He has given us the Holy Family: Jesus, Mary and Joseph, proof that the family unit was designed to give pure good and not evil. He has given us Jesus' words and example of how to love God and neighbor. He has given us living Beat-

---

2. To protect the privacy of interviewees, names have been changed where indicated with an asterisk.

itudes to bless our lives here and now and for the sake of God's eternal kingdom. Lupines grow and flourish on the slopes of devastation. Meals are made from ground seeds, crushed vegetables, humble water, and the belches of microorganisms.

Jesus rose from death out of barren rock. He makes all things new. He can — and has — filled your parenting pantry with good things. So let's open the door of that first pantry cabinet and see what's inside.

– 1 –

YOU SHALL LOVE THE LORD, YOUR GOD

With All Your Soul, and With All Your Mind

Beatitude Basic: Confidence

Those trusting in the LORD are like Mount Zion,
unshakable, forever enduring.

— Psalm 125:1

Rage, Roaches, and the Stamp of Providence

How do you love someone who has the power to make your life perfect but by all evidence has abandoned you to abuse, poverty, illness, and insult? How do you develop confidence in someone who allowed you to watch your mother get beaten by your father, your father lie to you in front of strangers just so he could keep a measly $4.50 in his pocket, and your mother spend hours in suicidal fits of rage-sobbing? How do you trust someone who let the infant you wake screaming in your crib, covered in roaches?[3]

Less suffering than this has turned countless others to atheism or at least agnosticism, saying, "No good god would permit me to feel this much pain." And yet, the child who experienced all this grew up to advise us, "Remember this one little truth: Nothing happens to you without the stamp of his providence placed upon it before it happens. That's faith."[4]

That's faith, indeed, according to Mother Angelica, foundress of EWTN. She suffered so much throughout her life, from her unstable childhood all the way to the stroke that took her mobility and her voice. Somehow, suffering became the engine of her faith rather than the death of it. Such faith gave Mother Angelica the confidence to build a worldwide evangelization network from next to nothing, a network that continued to grow even after she was no longer capable of running it and continues still, now that her earthly life has come to its end.

The faith that drove Mother Angelica is the same kind of faith necessary for cycle-breakers like us. The Christian family is just another type of evangelization network. We, too, cast out into the deep unknown of parenting in order to bring up a catch to give joy to God's kingdom. In a special way, we survivors of family abuse and dysfunction are like Mother Angelica in that we must build our networks from next to nothing as well. So how does the faith of a celibate nun who never parented an earthly soul in the traditional sense give us an example of the faith-born confidence we need as cycle-breaking parents? Like Mother Angelica, we need to love the God whose plans for us

---

3. Raymond Arroyo, *Mother Angelica: The Remarkable Story of a Nun, Her Nerve, and a Network of Miracles* (New York: Doubleday, 2005), 8–15.

4. EWTN Global Catholic Television Network, "Mother Mary Angelica," accessed February 16, 2021, http://www.ewtn.com/motherangelica/works.asp.

are exactly what we need. We need to believe in the plan God has to create something new and beautiful out of what earthly little we've been given. Unless we can believe that the intense suffering of our childhood was permitted for good and not evil, we as adult children and as parents ourselves will remain insecure, isolated in our own hurt. We will be unwilling to trust the good God to lead us. We instead will rail against the purposeless injustice of our childhood and grasp at every ephemeral parenting trend that comes our way, only to watch those trends disappear into failure, self-pity, and relationships broken on every side. Without a foundation of faith, our confidence in our choices as parents — and even in our choices as adult children of the parents we have — will flounder.

We cycle-breakers are being asked to take a huge leap of faith, a leap made larger and wider by our broken experiences of love. How do we make that leap into faith in a loving God when our formative experiences of trust were poisoned by the sins of those to whom our hearts had been entrusted — entrusted by God himself, no less? The people who were supposed to model God's love for us simply didn't. How do we pray "Our Father" when the very word "father" brings to mind memories of pain, or, because of abandonment, fails to conjure any image at all? How can we hear Jesus tell us from the cross, "Behold your mother," when the very word "mother" floods the memory with ridicule, blame, or helplessness in the face of that mother's rages? Faith is a gift. It's a hard one to ask for when we've been raised by parents who in fact do give their children snakes when they asked for fish (see Lk 11:11).

We are invited to love the Lord, our God, with all that we have, but we cannot love a God in whom we do not have faith, in whom we do not trust, in whom we have zero confidence. The *Catechism of the Catholic Church* tells us very early on that faith is a gift from God as well as a free choice.[5] That gift, when asked for, received, and chosen, turns our conversation with God from "How could you?" into a confident "Thank you."

The journey from raging agony to peace-filled gratitude is a long one. Thankfully, God promises that if we make that journey to him, he will break those cycles from which we are so hungry to escape, from which we are so eager to free our children. It's God's job to save us all, but as with all things God does, he longs to share that job with us. He's a bit like those good dads we see on TV, showing their kids how to repair the broken washing machine, or like the calm mom who teaches her kids how to scramble eggs, including how to pick out the bits of broken shell.

God wants us to be saved. He wants our children to be saved. He loves our parents enough to want them to be saved. Love of God gives us confidence that our past, present, and future are in the very best of hands. Here are some ways I've seen family abuse survivors, including myself, approach that place of healing love and confident trust.

Humans, We Have a Problem
We shouldn't be surprised that others' sins make it hard for us to see God's goodness. The first chapter of the Gospel of Mark reminds us that this is nothing new (see vv. 40–45). At the beginning of Jesus' ministry, he heals a leper and tells him not to tell anyone about it. What does the leper do? Obey out of gratitude? Of course not. He blabs all over town, so that the only way others can reach Jesus now is by following him out into the wilderness. He was healed, but he didn't trust Jesus' instructions; his disobedience made it difficult for others to reach Jesus. Our lives are no different. We must ask ourselves if we want healing badly enough to chase Jesus down for it. Remember, our world is a fallen one, and Jesus won't violate our defenses because he

---

5 . *Catechism of the Catholic Church*, 2nd ed. (Vatican: Libreria Editrice Vaticana, 2012), 150, 153.

loves us even when we throw them up in his face. When we go after Jesus because others' disobedience has pushed him from us, we test our intent and virtue. When we find him in truth, our purity of heart is proven — not to Jesus, who already knows it — but to us. That's the first step to confident, trusting love in God.

There's wisdom in the axiom, "The first step is admitting you have a problem." Sure, we know we don't want to do what our parents did. That's just the start of the battle. We must learn to embrace positive choices as much as turn away from negative ones. Like that leper, we must allow ourselves to be healed, and then we must obey Jesus' instructions in order to keep the path to him clear for our own children and others to approach him without obstacle. This is how we know that Jesus isn't being controlling when he tells us to show our love for him by keeping his commandments (see Jn 14:15). Our obedience to him above all other impulses — especially unhealthy impulses woven into us during our upbringing — is how we experience that trust that was missing in our broken relationships with our fallen parents. But how do we first learn to love the person who put us in the care of those fallen parents?

The key is in discovering the true personality of God. Of course, as God is infinitely immense, his personality is multi-dimensional, rich in aspects of longing to know and be known. God's is a personality of pure truth, truth that heals false beliefs and provides living examples of how to build reliable relationships where trust is earned, proven, and kept. He longs to show you the holes in his hands and feet and his wounded side. He makes himself vulnerable so we can trust that his plans are for our good. God is not afraid of our doubts.

As Christians, we believe God is a trinity of persons, three-in-one, Father, Son, and Holy Spirit; an ever-giving, ever-receiving community of persons who are separate but share all, give all, create all that is new and good. Man is made in the image and likeness of God. The family was created in the image and likeness of the Trinity. So man and the family would have continued had it not been for Adam and Eve, who not only brought sin into the world but also introduced each other and their children to blame, shame, denial, and all the maladaptive mental tricks that come with being a human in a fallen world (take a look at Genesis 3 if you need a refresher).

God the Father created us with the intention of perfection, knowing we would fall short, both as individuals and as families, but loving us into existence anyway. He knew we would suffer at one another's hands, even the hands of those he created to love us. Thus he knew he would have to send someone closely united with him — his Son, Jesus — to show us that suffering wasn't the perfect plan, but when rightly ordered it brings all our plans into God's perfection. This is the heart of the Incarnation: Jesus, God, took on human flesh so that he could give evidence that human problems were his problems too. God created us with free will, which by default includes the freedom to hate him, each other, and ourselves.

Yet in the Incarnation he shows that he did not abandon us to each other. He did not even abandon us to the idea that the dysfunctional family is the only kind of family there is. He could have sent his Son to us in any way he saw fit, but he chose the family unit: a child born to a woman and a man who'd united in self-sacrifice for the purpose of loving that child into adulthood and beyond. In our innocence as children, we were able to love selflessly the parents who mistreated us in their acquired lack of innocence. This then turned us, their victims, away from that innocence God had initially coded into us as children, into our parents when they were children — indeed, into the whole idea of family as modeled on the Holy Trinity. Pope Saint John Paul II described this reality in his 1981 apostolic exhortation *Familiaris Consortio* ("The Fellowship of the Family"). He wrote, "The Christian family, in fact, is the first community called to announce the Gospel to the human person during growth." He went on to explain that the family is the community first charged with the task of educating the child in "interpersonal relationships, rich in justice and in love."[6]

This is why family betrayal hurts so deeply. The family is the one thing we all have in common: In God's perfect will, we were destined for a loving one. The Incarnation, of course, is an acknowledgment that in our human willfulness (including the willfulness of the parents who've hurt us) we so often fall short of God's perfect will. If we didn't, we wouldn't have any need of the Incarnation.

Because God created us for pure, innocent, self-giving, all-receiving love, our failures and our parents' failures aren't just our problem. They're his too. God accepts that it's totally natural for our hearts to be broken by our parents' sins because they also break the heart of our heavenly Father. This is how we know God can empathize with us. He, too, has a heart weighed down by problems he neither caused nor asked for. He trusted the same people we trusted, and they failed us, and him. He longs for us to come to him so he can help us be for our own children what he wanted our parents to be for us.

In this, we have a credible opportunity for our wounded hearts to unite to God in the trust and love we did not get to experience with our earthly parents. He knows our pain because it is only a shadow of his. Thus we can believe that the good God is a loving Father, one who absolves false guilt rather than creating it. He heals rather than wounds. He shows us how holiness isn't just some intellectual exercise but it creates pure relationships safe from exploitation. And in our own growth in holiness, we don't just get to trust God — we experience the richness of God's trust in *us*.

We may struggle to see God's goodness, to trust in a God who

---

6. John Paul II, *Familiaris Consortio* (Vatican: Libreria Editrice Vaticana, 1981), par. 2.

would let these things happen to us. However, when we come seeking relationship with this God, no matter how hard that first step may be, we can at last receive the love that tells us we are wanted, that we belong, and that we matter. When we have that kind of relationship at last, we are better equipped to provide that for our own children. Confidence in our own worth and place in God's design thus takes root, grows, blossoms, and bears good fruit. By practicing trust in God, we go from being wounded creatures full of doubt, flailing around in search of the right thing to do by our innocent kids and by our parents, to the beloved children we were designed to be, returning trust for trust and love for love, just as we were created to do. This mysterious reciprocity equips us to form a new, peaceful, joyful family — because we're already participating in one with the best Father in the universe.

Such confidence is ours for the asking. It just takes practice.

God Absolves Us of False Guilt

One of the most terrifying moments of my life was the day I stood up to my mother. I was thirteen. It was newly spring. The windows were open, letting in a fresh breeze after a cool rain. I don't remember what brought it on, but I did something that bothered my mother, and I remember she lunged at me, reached between my breasts, pulled my bra strap from the front and then let it go. That was my punishment, justified in her eyes, and a punishment she doled out often at that phase of my life. I lunged back and started thumping my fists against her shoulders, screaming that I was going to report her to the police for child abuse. She, again being justified in her own eyes, yelled back that she was going to report me for parental abuse.

My fists froze. She got me to stop punching her, all right.

I don't remember how many weeks or months I spent wondering if she actually would call the police. Would I go to court, to juvenile hall? Would they just let me off with probation? Did I even know what probation was? What if the neighbors had heard (the windows had been open, after all) and were going to report me? Or what if someone, unlikely as it was, believed my side of the story, and my mother got sent to jail and I to a foster home? My already bad sleeping patterns worsened. Suicidal thoughts, which had haunted me since I was eight years old, seemed to peer around every corner of my brain. When would my guilt be discovered?

The day came that God let me discover that such "guilt" was not mine to carry. As a young adult, when I turned my life over to Christ, I just sent up the plea, "God or whoever you are, show me the truth, no matter how difficult it is." God answered first with the truth that is so obvious it's what we call natural law. The *Catechism* explains, "The natural law expresses the original moral sense which enables man to discern by reason the good and the evil, the truth and the lie" (1954). We don't need a Bible to tell us that parents should take care of their children, not humiliate them. Even the sparrows in their nests know how to take care of their young. That order is only interrupted when we humans dis-order it in order to give ourselves false comfort in the moment.

Truth outlasts moments. Truth showed me that when I stood up to that one moment of abuse, I was setting a boundary that I, as a unique and precious child of God, had every right to set. In fact, I shouldn't have needed to set it had my mother chosen to discipline me with patience and understanding rather than rage and degradation. What made her sin worse, though, for both my growing psyche and, ultimately, her conscience, is that when she was confronted with her failure, instead of admitting her wrong and repairing the damage she'd done, she convinced me that her guilt was mine. I still wonder if she really thought I was the one at fault there, or was that just her fallen response to the pain of her conscience? Was she so afraid of the pain of being wrong that she had to convince herself, and by extension her teenage daughter, that she was right, perfect, beyond any kind of reproach?

Only God can know her mind or the mind of any of our parents.

I hope you can see in this story just one instance of the false guilt that we humans can place on each other. Ever since that one breezy time of day, when Adam and Eve tried using paradise to hide from God, most people confronted with the pain of their own evil are desperate to deny it. The more innocent and vulnerable we are, the more likely we are to buy into another sinner's lies. What's worse, we then become more likely to thrust our own actual guilt onto others because that's how we were taught to handle a painful conscience: Pass it on. Passing it on, alas, doesn't make it go away. It only makes it fester in two hearts: that of the sinner and, often enough, the heart of an innocent child.

That breezy day when I was thirteen was, indeed, harrowing, but it was also a gift that God left me so that, when I had reattached myself to truth, who is Jesus, I could see that I was not the one at fault. That guilt was not mine. I could let it go and free myself to work on my own actual sins. As another axiom goes, "Hurt people hurt people," so there are plenty of my own sins for me to face. You can be free to do the same. Cling to truth, no matter how scary or painful it is, and you can only be clinging to the good, holy, unfailing perfection that is the eternal love of Christ. Cling to truth, and you will be confident in your choices with your own children. That's how love of God builds up the brokenhearted parent.

Loving God Heals

The guilt of abuse against us is not ours to bear. The next leap of faith we must take is that it's not God's either. I don't know about you, but this remains my biggest struggle: How can I trust a God who let these things happen to me? Doesn't a good father protect his children? If God did not protect me, how am I supposed to pray a single Our Father, much less six of them every day on a rosary, not to mention all those Hail Marys, celebrating the love of a perfect mother, who, by the way, could have interceded for me and asked God to keep me from the pain my own very imperfect mother inflicted upon me? I mean,

I know that without free will our love for God would be worthless. Without sinful choices available to us, there's no virtue in choosing the good. So then, why do I still have this wound, this tendency to disbelieve that God has good plans for me, plans for hope and other good things, as he promises in Jeremiah 29:11–13: "For I know well the plans I have in mind for you — oracle of the LORD — plans for your welfare and not for woe, so as to give you a future of hope. When you call me, and come and pray to me, I will listen to you. When you look for me, you will find me. Yes, when you seek me with all your heart."

I have this tendency not to trust what is true because humans more powerful than I was at the time used their power to warp my sense of what is real. This obscured my ability to see through their sinfulness and, thus, make them feel pain they were desperate to avoid — so desperate that they would misshape an innocent child's mind in order to do so. But again, God is truth. Yes, he allowed us all our childhood agonies, but he also allowed his own Son Jesus to die — beaten, humiliated, stripped, and hung on a cross in front of a derisive public. Jesus endured every kind of abuse there is in the crucifixion. Because of the mysterious nature of the Trinity, because of the very nature of love, I wonder if all three persons of God shared deeply and intimately in that pain. For years, I meditated on this reality and still found myself asking, "God, you gave my parents free will, and they used that gift to crush me. You allowed this. If I, in my pathetic humanity, want to repair the damage my choices have allowed, and if your love is supposed to be perfect, *shouldn't you want to make this up to me?*"

It was an arrogant question. Thankfully, God is never afraid of arrogance. He doesn't need to be. Instead I discovered the answer to my demand in the crucifixion itself. He *did* make it up to me — to us all. Jesus shows us that pain from others' sins against us is not the end. Showing others the reality of the suffering they have caused us, and facing ourselves the reality of suffering we have caused others, sets us free. This is truth: By his cross and resurrection, he sets us free.

God did not want these things to happen to us. Our earthly parents did. The guilt of abuse is not ours, but neither is it God's. God may have allowed our pain, but he also redeems it. He may not have protected me from my parents's sins, but in showing me that truth, no matter how painful, is the path to heaven, he protects me from the eternal pains of hell. My future can be different because I am perfectly loved by God, no matter how imperfectly people love me and no matter how imperfectly I love them. I am not doomed to repeat the unloving mistakes imperfect people taught me. I have been taught by Christ, the great teacher, who shows each of us that we don't have to die the deaths that previous generations chose. Through our crosses, perhaps *because of* our crosses, we can choose life for ourselves and, best of all, our descendants after us.

Our parents's sins are not the end of our story.

Holiness Helps in the Here and Now

Once we are able to trust (or at least work on trusting) the true God who selflessly loves us, it's a lot clearer that pursuit of a relationship with him doesn't just heal the past. It paves a path through the present into a future that leads to eternity, not just for ourselves but for our own children. Let's take a look at Matthew 15:29–37. First, Jesus led over four thousand people out to the middle of the mountainous wilderness. Matthew tells us that, "Great crowds came to him, having with them the lame, the blind, the deformed, the mute, and many others. They placed them at his feet, and he cured them." He also preached to the people. So he does this, the preaching and the healing, for three whole days. Then … surprise! They all ran out of food. On top of that, they'd been led away from civilization, away from all the support that those who hadn't followed Jesus still had on hand. And what does Jesus do? He took what little they had away from them! The gall of this guy, right? Of course, we know what happened. Jesus took those seven loaves (probably stale by that point) and two fish (probably starting to turn a bit fishy, pun intended), and he turned them into abundance for thousands and thousands of people and their children.

What lesson does this teach you and me? We follow Jesus even though we are broken. He heals us. He teaches us. But he often chooses to do those things for us out in the desert. Why? Because he wants us to know that he is trustworthy, even when our lives seem as barren as the blast zone around Mount Saint Helens. If we hand over what we have, he will increase it, and we will have more than we need. What little we have is already his anyway. When we accept that truth, which is the same truth that sets us free from false guilt and empowers us to repair the damage that our own sins have caused, we are confirmed in our freedom. We grow in trust. We align ourselves with the steady truth that is God's love. God's faithful love is what we deserved as children. God's faithful love is what our own children deserve now. Pursuing that love gives us the confidence that all things shall be well. God makes new all that comes from our past, our present experience, and all that is to come in our families' futures. When we at last believe that our pain can be redeemed into something new, we live with a joyful confidence, knowing that nothing bad will last, and no one can steal God's goodness from its tabernacle inside our hearts.

Why all this emphasis here on holiness instead of just plain mental health? Holiness is just an old-fashioned word for the pursuit of God who is truth. When we follow Jesus into even the most barren places, he teaches us, he heals us, and he even feeds us real food — nourishment for us to share with our own children. That nourishment is love. Secular self-help books can be great for learning healthy mental habits and parenting techniques. Alas, they simply aren't designed to sustain us like a relationship with Jesus does. The best part of aiming for holiness rather than the parenting trend *du jour* is that doing so ensures consistency and makes us people our kids can rely on. They might not like what we say, but they'll know they can rely on us to be a solid rock in the ever-shifting sea that is our fallen world.

This gives us confidence in ourselves, and it gives our children reason to have their own confidence in us.

This is where prayer, Christian meditation, and the sacraments come in. These disciplines teach us to listen not just *to* the truth but *for* the truth. Prayer, meditation, and the sacraments shape us to be silent, to see false guilt for what it is, and to see our own sins for what they are, so that we can make reparation to our children when we hurt them, thereby breaking that cycle of passing on sins that we're too afraid to face. You want to break the cycle of dysfunctional families? Pursue truth. Pursue Christ. Pursue holiness. Pursue the love of God. Pursuit of that which cannot change strengthens the foundation of your relational and parenting confidence.

God Trusts You, Too

Let's face it: If God is all-powerful, he has the power to make our lives a living hell. It's easy to assume that he did, when we ourselves were taught to deny reality in order to see past the myriad ways others were hurting us for their own immediate gratification. Yet when we pursue the truth, who is Christ, into all kinds of wilderness, we can be just like Mother Angelica and see the stamp of God's provision on every hurt, every cross we've ever borne.

Faith like Mother Angelica's, necessarily builds on trust, which then builds up love. There will be days when the memories make us question ourselves, when our own failures at parenting make us question our worth, when faith, trust, and love are all so hard to come by. Dawn Eden, a Catholic convert, author, and survivor of childhood sexual abuse and paternal neglect, writes, "It is not essential that I *feel* loved by God. What matters most is that I accept the undeniable facts of my birth and continued existence as evidence that he cares about me, sustains me, and therefore must have a purpose for me."[7] We abuse survivors have been taught to doubt reality. When we make the

---

7. Dawn Eden, *My Peace I Give You: Healing Sexual Wounds With the Help of the Saints* (Notre Dame: Ave Maria Press, 2012), 39.

choice to pursue truth through holiness, we rebuild faith, hope, love, and trust every time it feels like we've lost them.

Yes, God did let sin into the world, but only as part of allowing us the freedom to choose a relationship with reality — with him. Some of us choose otherwise. If you have this book in your hands, though, it's a testament to the truth that in spite of what your parents may have done to you, and even in spite of what sins you may have committed against your own children, you want reality. You don't want to hide from God anymore and kid yourself that the disconnection you feel is paradise. You're ready to pursue holiness and let it lead you to becoming a better, more truth-filled, more loving parent. In that truth, no matter how broken our hearts may be, we have access to unshakable joy.

God's love is eternal, whether we have faith in him or not. It stands to reason that, if we cultivate our faith as Mother Angelica did, we align ourselves with the unfailing, unconditional love that promises to make good of our past hurts and build an unshakable foundation for our children's future. Modeling ourselves after that love brings healing to all of us living in this fallen world. Even with God's help we're still going to mess up. God trusts us with the gift of free will. Yes, he asks us to trust him, but he also trusts us with the pain he's allowed, with our own sins, and with the precious hearts of our children. A heart that puts God first is predisposed to the truth. When we readily accept the true, we are more welcoming of the dignity of the other person. This is where the pursuit of holiness leads us to love our neighbor, whether those neighbors are our children, our parents, or even the broken, sinful, sinned-against neighbor in the mirror.

HOLY FAMILY MOMENT
The Annunciation (Lk 1:26-38)
God started the perfect earthly family by asking Mary to do some-

thing that had never been done before. She did not know if her parents would support her. She did not know if she would survive the pregnancy or the birth. She did not know whether Joseph would stand with her or abandon her. She was embarking on a journey chosen for her by God, but it was a journey that would expose her to ridicule, shame, condemnation, and abandonment by others.

She said yes anyway. Faith led her to an unshakable confidence. Her perfect confidence shows us how a loving parent relies on God's providence to lead our children into eternal life.

BEATITUDE BASIC WORKSHOP
Confidence

1. Break out your journal and write down one thing about which you feel guilty from your childhood. First, pray that Jesus sheds the light of truth on you as you fearlessly examine your guilty feelings. Write down reasons why this guilt might truly be yours. Then write down reasons why this guilt might rightfully belong to someone who hurt you. Repeat this exercise with one thing about which you feel guilty from your parenting choices. What is God teaching you through these guilty feelings?

2. Truth is unchanging. If it changes, it's not truth. Pursue truth, even when it hurts. Clinging to truth is the most concrete way to love God with all our hearts, souls, and minds. Write five things in your journal that you know to be unchangeably true. Then write five things you want to believe are true but have trouble trusting that they are. Invite God into these doubts. He is not afraid of them.

3. Truth leads us to obey God and not the whims of fallen humans. Pursue truth for both healing and for

guidance in what choices to make, both in our relationships with our own children and in our relationships with our parents. Journal about one personal whim you have followed. Did it lead you to or away from truth?

_____

LITANY OF TRUST

From the belief that I have to earn Your love, deliver me, Jesus.

From the fear that I am unlovable, deliver me, Jesus.

From the false security that I have what it takes, deliver me, Jesus.

From the fear that trusting you will leave me more destitute, deliver me, Jesus.

From all suspicion of your words and promises, deliver me, Jesus.

From the rebellion against childlike dependency on you, deliver me, Jesus.

From refusals and reluctances in accepting your will, deliver me, Jesus.

From anxiety about the future, deliver me, Jesus.

From resentment or excessive preoccupation with the past, deliver me, Jesus.

From restless self-seeking in the present moment, deliver me, Jesus.

From disbelief in your love and presence, deliver me, Jesus.

From the fear of being asked to give more than I have, deliver me, Jesus.

From the belief that my life has no meaning or worth, deliver me, Jesus.

From the fear of what love demands, deliver me, Jesus.

From discouragement, deliver me, Jesus.

That you are continually holding me, sustaining me, loving me, Jesus, I trust in you.

That your love goes deeper than my sins and failings, and transforms me, Jesus, I trust in you.

That not knowing what tomorrow brings is an invitation to lean on
   you, Jesus, I trust in you.
That you are with me in my suffering, Jesus, I trust in you.
That my suffering, united to your own, will bear fruit in this life and
   the next, Jesus, I trust in you.
That you will not leave me orphan, that you are present in your
   Church, Jesus, I trust in you.
That your plan is better than anything else, Jesus, I trust in you.
That you always hear me, and in Your goodness always respond to
   me, Jesus, I trust in you.
That you give me the grace to accept forgiveness and to forgive oth-
   ers, Jesus, I trust in you.
That you give me all the strength I need for what is asked, Jesus, I
   trust in you.
That my life is a gift, Jesus, I trust in you.
That you will teach me to trust You, Jesus, I trust in you.
That you are my Lord and my God, Jesus, I trust in you.
That I am your beloved one, Jesus, I trust in you.
Amen.

— *Sister Faustina Maria Pia, Sister of Life*[8]

SAINT-SPIRATION
Saint Thomas Aquinas

When we think of Aquinas, we tend to picture an intellectual gi-
ant who wrote dry, inaccessible philosophy. I know I did, anyway,
when I tried reading the *Summa Theologiae* before I actually got
to know the writer himself.

   Thomas was born into a wealthy family of Italian nobles, and
boy, did they have big plans for their eighth child: Surely he'd be-

---

8. Faustina Maria Pia, "Litany of Trust," Sisters of Life, accessed February 16, 2021, https://sistersoflife
.org/wp-content/uploads/2019/05/Mobile-Litany-of-Trust-English-1.pdf. Used with permission from
the Sisters of Life. Prayer cards of the Litany of Trust are available for personal use at SistersofLife.org.

come the abbot at a comfortable Benedictine monastery. When Thomas showed preference for a new begging order called the Dominicans, Thomas's mother especially would have none of it. Thomas pursued God's call over his family of origin's demands, however, and he joined the Dominicans in secret. When word got back to his family, his mother sent two of her other sons with some armed men to kidnap Thomas and bring him back home.

Over the next year, his family did everything they could to tempt him away from his vocation. At one point, they disregarded his boundaries so viciously that they sent a prostitute into his room to seduce him. He famously chased her out of the castle with a hot metal poker. Thomas's resolve in all things was stronger than his family's. They finally let him go back to the Dominicans, but his mother told all her friends that he had run away again. Thomas Aquinas, Doctor of the Church, knew the pain of a parent's blame-shifting.

Like us, Saint Thomas knows what it's like to have a family that loves appearances more than truth. In this, Saint Thomas also shows us how to cling to God's love in spite of that betrayal.[9]

9. Biography.com Editors, "Saint Thomas Aquinas Biography," The Biography.com website, updated September 10, 2020, https://www.biography.com/religious-figure/saint-thomas-aquinas.

– 2 –
YOU SHALL LOVE YOUR NEIGHBOR AS YOURSELF

Beatitude Basic: Compassion

Even if my father and mother forsake me,
the LORD will take me in.
LORD, show me your way;
lead me on a level path
because of my enemies.

— Psalm 27:10–11

Learning What We Lived

When I was a child, there was a poem framed on the wall of my aunt's powder room. The title was "Children Learn What They Live."[10] I was no more than seven years old, and I would stand on tiptoe to read the poem as I washed my hands.

> If children live with criticism, they learn to condemn.
> If children live with hostility, they learn to fight. ...
> If children live with ridicule, they learn to feel shy.

The first half of the poem was filled with such lines. Jealousy begets envy, shame begets guilt, and so on. It all made sense, even to my childish mind. After all, I was constantly ridiculed for being shy, felt nonstop guilt, withered with envy under comparisons to my far more personable older brother, and that was just for starters. The second half of the poem, however, baffled me. It baffled me just as much as reading another piece of inspirational wall art, this one at my pediatrician's office. That one bore a title promising it would teach the reader how to be more hypocritical, which I was pretty sure was a bad thing, but that didn't match with its promises to practice art in rightness and honor. (I was a precocious reader at seven, but my knowledge had not yet included the differentiation between the words "hypocrite" and "Hippocratic.")

Anyway, back to the second half of "Children Learn What They Live," the half that baffled me. It spoke of how to teach children good things like appreciation, love, and justice by showing them praise, acceptance, and fairness. I wondered why my aunt had hung this on a wall when she and her sister, my mother, hadn't seemed to have read the second half of the poem. Why were they teaching us, their children, these bad things and not teaching us the good ones from the poem's second half?

---

10. Dorothy Law Nolte and Rachel Harris, *Children Learn What They Live: Parenting to Inspire Values* (New York: Workman Publishing, 1998), vi–vii.

I was legitimately confused. My confusion was a testament to the disconnect between the natural law that is written on the human heart, and what I lived in the day-to-day experience of being raised by, not to put too fine a point on it, unrepentant sinners. These unrepentant sinners shelled out good money to send me to Catholic schools and took the time to bring me to Sunday Mass. At both places I heard, "Love your neighbor." Still a dependent child, I had to return home with those unrepentant sinners. In my innocence, I recognized that something was wrong, even if I couldn't name it, even if I couldn't identify its remedy. I knew — no, I *ached* — to become those good things the poem mentioned: confident, patient, generous, loving, and friendly. I also instinctively recognized that I was not being taught those things. If children learned what they lived, where would I learn to be good? Where would I learn to become lovable and how to love in return?

As always, God has good news for all of us, even those of us raised with hostility, ridicule, and shame — even for the very people who raised us that way, and especially for the children we are raising with our own fallen ways of doing this parenting thing. We've already talked about the requirement to love God with all we have. As Jesus says in Matthew 22:34–40, the single greatest commandment is actually two. Loving God is one thing. Loving our neighbor is something else. Because the two are actually one great commandment, Jesus makes it pretty clear that we aren't loving God unless we also love the people he put in our lives. In equal measures, Jesus places love of neighbor next to "as yourself." By juxtaposing both kinds of human love, Jesus makes it clear that godly love of neighbor cannot obliterate love of self, nor can love of self excuse us from loving our neighbor. They are one in the same. In other words, you can't love your neighbor unless you have one.

God has designed family to provide us with our first set of

neighbors. Those of us who go on to build families of our own thus become the first set of neighbors for the next generation. God meant for this closeness to foster compassion, but we all know how short we humans fall of that plan — some of us farther than others. Wherever we are in our own neighborhoods, between the sins of our parents and the strivings of our innocent children, the confidence that comes from learning to love God first creates an environment of confidence inside even the most wounded heart. That is where love of the other, because of a new love of the self, can take root, grow, blossom, and plant seeds to nourish God's gift of children to us.

First, however, for the sake of those children and our wounded but lovable selves, we have a lot of new life to live because we come to parenting with a whole lot to learn.

Welcome to the Neighborhood

Patricia* grew up in the 1970s and '80s in what anyone in their small evangelical church would have called a "good family." She, her brother, and her parents all were active in church leadership and community service. She remembers no physical abuse at home, no substance abuse, no sexual impropriety of any kind. Her parents didn't even smoke, even in those days when the surgeon general was just starting to put warning labels on cigarettes. Still, she says, "There was a shadow in my life that I couldn't quite put my finger on."

As an adult, she now can see how her parents' behavior cast that shadow. Her mother would rain down verbal abuse at her for failing to meet her housekeeping expectations — expectations that were unreasonable for an adult, much less twelve-year-old Patty. Her father would rage at Patty and anyone else who ever made him wait for any amount of time. Christmas and birthdays in her household were the stuff of nightmares. As they gave Patty her gifts, her parents coldly informed her, "You're not worth it."

After years of this, one Christmas, a teenaged Patty replied, "Take it back then. If I'm not worth it, you shouldn't have bought it." Rather than address their daughter's obvious hurt by taking responsibility for their cruelty, both of her parents accused her of ruining Christmas for everyone. It's no wonder she felt she always had to be on guard. She says, "I learned to take the emotional temperature of a room before I entered it or before I spoke, because I wasn't sure that I could safely express myself. And there was a chronic question that haunted me, even when it wasn't asked out loud. 'What have you been doing? What have you accomplished?'"

Patricia's story shows us that parents don't have to hit a child to hurt a child. "Now," Patricia says, "thanks to my counselor, my research, my constant crying out to God, I can see that no matter what my parents say, they do not love me. They have never loved me. What they love is the ability to control me."

What Patricia describes is called *enmeshment*, and that is the name of the poison that twists parental love into destruction. The psychological term *enmeshment* has a lot of lingo around it, mostly relying on terms like "diffused boundaries" and "loss of autonomous development." The cleanest definition I've found for enmeshment, however, is simply this: Enmeshment is taking things too personally. While that may sound oversimplified, if we extrapolate we can see how enmeshment works on almost any level. Enmeshment is a thirst for control. It lies to us that we have control over another person, and therefore we have a right to exert that control, to make sure that person makes us feel better, no matter the truth of our actions.

Enmeshment tells a father that he can make himself feel better by raging at his child, no matter how much it hurts the child, but it also tells that child that he can control Dad's rages by hiding in his room. An enmeshed mother thinks to herself, "I can guarantee my son's future by selecting all his college courses for him, whether he likes it or not." An enmeshed daughter thinks, "I can control my mom's drinking by faking sick so she can't go to the bar." Even a well-meaning parent can become enmeshed by avoiding any conflict that causes her child any kind of upset — upset that teaches a child his limits and his ability to persevere. Bottom line: An enmeshed parent thinks, "This child exists to make me feel better, so I can treat or ignore this child in any way that I wish, and there will be no consequences."

The consequences, however, are soul-crushing, to both the child *and the parent*. Enmeshment can infect any relationship with the poison of false control, and wherever truth does not reign, hearts cannot truly connect with each other. Catholic therapist Dr. Greg Popcak describes how enmeshment plays out by saying, "Enmeshed parents are so concerned that their child will do the wrong thing, get the wrong answer, or attempt to do things the wrong way that they are constantly intervening whether their kids need it or not or want it or not."[11] However, until a parent honors a child's unique identity as a child of God first, and a gift to said parent second, that parent-child relationship will be based on delusions of false other-control; it will not be based on self-giving, other-honoring love. We cannot know and be known unless we recognize our separateness from our neighbors and our neighbors' separateness from us.

Patricia saw this in her own family growing up. When she looks at her mother's housekeeping demands, she says, "I learned pretty quick that it was better to do the work than hear that sharp, hateful voice of my mother." On those rare times her mother doled out showy praise for her daughter's efforts, Patricia says, "There was this sickening feeling about those words. I didn't do them for that praise, and I never could figure out why her 'thanks' didn't satisfy me. I see now it was because those words declared her victory. She had won the game. She knew that she could bully me into

11. Dr. Gregory K. Popcak, "Honey Don'ts and Helicopters," CatholicCounselors.com, accessed February 16, 2021, catholiccounselors.com/honey-donts-and-helicopters/.

working around the house. And I never said no to her. I never did those things out of love. I did them out of fear. My heart was empty toward her, so it's no wonder I found no joy in her false praise."

Patricia's mother, like so many of our own parents, punished her child through wrath because she did not see that Patricia was an independent child of God, gifted with free will. I'm not saying parents shouldn't try to keep their children under control when age-appropriate, but this can only be accomplished effectively by teaching the child to cultivate her own internal self-control. Love begets obedience to God, but obedience is not in and of itself love. Patricia's mother did not recognize her daughter as separate from her and thus could not see her as a neighbor to love. She only saw her as a thing to control, step on, and compete with for power. This made it nigh impossible for Patricia to love her mother spontaneously in return.

Of course, with God, all things are possible, but as Jesus spent most of the New Testament telling the Pharisees, God's ways are not our ways. How godly love is going to look between you and your family of origin might not be what you expect — or what they demand. How godly love will look between you and your children may also be surprising to you. However, choosing how to love our families of origin in truth and not mere appeasement is critical to being present in full, godly love, not just to our own children but to ourselves. We must learn to navigate how to say both our "yes" and our "no" in love on both sides of the generational divide over which we cycle-breakers must straddle. It's a good thing for us that God knows exactly how to do that and is eager to show us how. When we give ourselves to him in pursuit of holiness, he uses our crosses to bring the joy of life back to our broken families.

Good Fences, Good Neighbors
When I'm getting a bit dressed up for church, work, or date night, I like to accessorize a bit. I have a special hanger in my

closet that is made up of a dozen or so hooks hanging down from a horizontal bar. I put my scarves, belts, and even some larger, chunky necklaces on it. I *like* to accessorize. What I *don't* like to do is stop every time I'm getting undressed for the night and hang each scarf and necklace on its proper hook. I'm tired. I just want to plop whatever accessory of which I'm divesting myself onto the nearest hook. So I do. Of course, you don't need a degree in physics to know that, if all the belts, scarves and necklaces are hung on the very last hook on the bar, the bar is going to tip over, and all those lovely accessories are going to end up on the closet floor in a tangled heap. I can't wear them again until I spend time scooping them up off the floor, disentangling them from each other, then hanging them properly, like I should have in the first place, on their individual hooks, spaced evenly across the bar. When I deny each item its proper place, I buy myself maybe three seconds of extra sleep with what will be fifteen minutes of cleanup. Scarves and necklaces *really* like to tangle, and I've even broken a few of my less sturdy necklaces in such falls.

Dr. Henry Cloud and Dr. John Townsend are famous for their *Boundaries* series. For those of you unfamiliar with their work, they write, "Boundaries define us. They define what is me and what is not me. A boundary shows me where I end and someone else begins, leading me to a sense of ownership. Knowing what I am to own and take responsibility for gives me freedom."[12] Another word for boundaries? *Truth.* It's really that simple. You are not your neighbor. Your neighbor is not you. You each are responsible for your own choices. Just like my accessories will fare better if I take the effort to put them on their own hooks, when we identify the parts of our relationships we can't control, we stop fighting against reality. We stop putting

---

12. Henry Cloud and John Townsend, *Boundaries: When to Say Yes, When to Say No, to Take Control Of Your Life* (Grand Rapids: Zondervan, 1992), 29.

all our neighbors on the same hook and making a mess of our relationships.

If love is, as we understand it according to Saint Thomas Aquinas, "to wish [a person] good things,"[13] or more common-ly, "to will the good of the other," then love of neighbor means making choices that don't deny what is good: the truth. Each of us is, as Charlotte's Brontë's heroine Jane Eyre says, "a free human being with an independent will." The good of the other, of all of us, is union with God, up to and eventually including heaven. We love our neighbor when we don't stand in the way of his getting to heaven. We also love our neighbor when we don't try to drag him to heaven against his own will. Most of all, we love both our neighbor and ourselves when we make of our own choices a signpost to the eternal love of the triune God. This is the kind of love you can show anyone: your distractible child, your abusive mother, your sullen spouse, even the truck driver who nearly ran you off the road. Boundaries allow us to love by choice, the way God loves us, and not by fear of reprisal, the way Patricia's parents and yours and mine tried to make us love them. Actually, what they demanded wasn't love; it was ap-peasement. The two are not the same thing.

So in our relationships, especially with our families of or-igin and with our children, we show godly love by accepting the fact that we can't force anyone to behave in a way that will make us feel good. That's the essence of having healthy bound-aries. Mental and spiritual freedom come from not allowing the choices of others to constrain our choices, either before or after we make them. This means you have the right to tell people not to sin against you and to choose consequences when they do. Patricia had the right to point out her parents' cruelty to her. When at thirteen I stood up to my mother, I had a right to

---

13. Thomas Aquinas, *Summa Theologiae*, I-II, q.26, a.4, NewAdvent.org, http://www.newadvent.org /summa/3026.htm#article6.

tell her that snapping my bra strap was wrong and that I was allowed to seek protection from such treatment.

You have a right to tell your parents that they are not permitted to sin against you either. How they react is their problem. If you do not practice this truth in your life, you run the risk of not letting your children live the things they need to learn, the appreciation, love, and justice, and more named in that poem. Our children cannot learn to love and appreciate the other if they can't distinguish between self and other. If we are to teach them this type of true, compassionate love, we must live it ourselves first.

After a lifetime of enmeshment and poor boundaries, you may read this and start to panic and say, "Of course other people's choices are my problem! My parents will put consequences on *me* if I dare to tell them they're wrong. My children will hate *me* if I try to love them this way!"

These are totally understandable fears. To most of us survivors of family abuse, setting boundaries probably looks like, well, the sin of selfishness. After all, Saint Paul tells us in 1 Corinthians 13 that love "does not seek its own interests," right? In fact, you may have told an abusive family member that you would no longer sit by and let them hurt you anymore, and they came back with, "Turn the other cheek!" "Honor your father and mother!" "That's parent abuse!" or "That's not very Christian of you to talk to me like that!" And those are the messages we have replaying inside of our heads whenever we have to tell our children "no." Many of us have come to parenting with the fear that there is something inherently wrong in standing up for ourselves.

What we need to discover, in order to approach the word "no" with vital compassion, is that God doesn't ask us to stand up for *ourselves*. He asks us to stand up for the *truth*. He asks us to stand up for him.

In fact, one of the most courageously compassionate things

we can do is to tell people that they've sinned. Hard to believe, isn't it? Let's go back and read Matthew 9:2 (the healing of a paralytic), Mark 2:5 (the healing of another paralytic, this one lowered through the roof), Luke 7:48 (the woman washing Jesus' feet with her tears), John 8:1–11 (the woman caught in adultery), and, one of my favorites, John 9:41, where Jesus heals the man born blind, but tells the Pharisees that their sin remains because they insist that they couldn't possibly be blind themselves in any way. Do you see a pattern in those stories, where Jesus talks about sin to the sinners? He discusses people's sin, but he always does so in terms of forgiveness and healing. Those who, like the Pharisees, refuse to admit that they have sinned, are left blind and paralyzed, at least spiritually.

Of course, when Jesus calls out the Pharisees for blinding themselves to their own sins, he shows us that we are to admit our own sins first (see Matthew 7:5). This only reinforces the compassion aspect of talking about sin. A compassionate adult knows it's hard to face sin, but he also has experienced the freedom that comes from facing sin in order to accept forgiveness from a loving God. The confidence that comes from loving God gives us the grace to confront our worst selves. Then compassion demands that we point others toward that freedom, no matter how much doing so might scare us.

As our own wounds tell us, children need compassionate adults. To become compassionate for your children's sake if not your own, you must first get comfortable confronting your own sin rather than staying a willfully blind Pharisee. This will help you let your children see you as a fellow human capable of surviving big emotions and big mistakes — even their big emotions and mistakes. Then, when it's time to confront their sins with discipline, you'll not only have shown them how a person faces that particular music, but you'll also have shown them that you're their ally, not their adversary, in the good fight. You'll be handing them tools from their own heart to create their own boundaries, their own healthy ability of knowing when to say "yes" or "no," especially to themselves. God will be using you as his invitation to them to experience the joy of being made new.

If you're worried that setting boundaries — with your parents, your children, or just with anyone at all — is a selfish way to destroy your relationships rather than a healthy way to heal them, bring that worry to Jesus. Jesus, the Prince of Peace, is also the King of Boundaries. Mark 1:35, Matthew 14:23, Luke 6:12, and Luke 22:41 all show us the different ways he went off by himself to pray in solitude rather than being at people's constant beck and call. In Mark 3:7–12, Jesus asks the disciples to have a boat ready for him so he can escape the crush of the crowds that have come to demand his healing touch. If Jesus, in all his compassion and mercy, can have boundaries, so can we.

Best of all, for those of us looking to establish healthier boundaries between ourselves and our parents and our children, both Jesus and Mary, his mother, honored each others' boundaries. In Chapter 2 of John's Gospel, Jesus and Mary pop on down to Cana for a wedding. When the wine runs out, Mary simply tells the truth: "They have no wine." Jesus responds by pointing out the boundary between himself, her, and even the couple hosting the wedding: "Woman, how does your concern affect me? My hour has not yet come." Mary doesn't rage or smack him or even guilt her son into doing what she wants. She simply tells the servants the best advice anyone could give: "Do whatever he tells you."

And they do. And his wine is way better than the old stuff. So it will be in our lives when we commit to living like Jesus and Mary did, with honesty about what we have a duty to control, with courage to surrender over those things we can't. I'm no theologian, but I'm willing to bet that Jesus is the Prince of Peace *because* he's the King of Boundaries.

Mending Fences

So boundaries are good and godly, not sinful or selfish. Fine. But just because Jesus was able to set and keep boundaries doesn't mean we'll have an easy time doing so, especially when our parents, the people who were supposed to teach us that truth, worked so hard to poison it out of us — so hard that we may face our own children with fear rather than compassion. Jesus is God, omniscient and omnipotent. We're just slobs in a fallen world, and we need remedial lessons in reality. Where can *we* begin?

The basic idea of setting true, healthy boundaries is identifying the truth in a relationship and making choices that honor that truth. Therefore, you need to begin identifying your boundaries by identifying the truth: the reality of where you end and your neighbor (parent, child, spouse, or literal neighbor) begins. If we believe that Jesus is the truth, then Jesus is in the reality that exists within us and without.

Here is a by no means exhaustive list of reality of what exists within me:

- My thoughts
- My feelings
- My actions
- My attitudes
- My speech
- My gestures
- My fears
- My preferences
- My sins

These things are my responsibility and nobody else's. Some of them, like my words, gestures, and actions, including my sins, are completely under my control. Some of them, like my thoughts, feelings, and attitudes, may come to me unbidden, but they remain my responsibility. For example, if I have lustful thoughts about someone not my spouse, then it's my job to school my mind to redirect my imagination to something that is good and true, such as owning the reality of whatever troubles I may be having with my spouse that are tempting me to mental escapism. It would be easy to say, "If he hadn't been being such a jerk, I wouldn't be thinking about someone else!" The harsh but solid reality? If all were smooth sailing between me and the hubby, I wouldn't be hiding from the discord between us by thinking about someone else. Our thoughts, feelings and attitudes may be out of our immediate control, but they are the messages God sends from within us to help us find those areas we need to bring to him for healing, especially when our fears prevent us from seeing a clear way through.

Speaking of those fears, if you're reading this book, chances are you grew up in an enmeshed relationship with at least one parent. This means that parent did a good job of convincing you of the destructive lie that you are responsible for:

- Others' thoughts
- Others' feelings
- Others' actions
- Others' attitudes
- Others' speech
- Others' gestures
- Others' fears
- Others' preferences
- Others' sins

Remember Patricia's mother screaming at her daughter for not keeping house "properly"? She was trying to make young Patty responsible for her own sin of sloth. Remember her parents telling her that she wasn't worth her Christmas and birthday gifts? They were trying to make their daughter responsible for their ingratitude for the gift of her in their lives. They were wrong to do so.

"What I had thought all along was duty and love toward them was nothing but me feeding [my parents'] self-obsession. In return I was given anxiety, depression, low self-esteem, high blood pressure, and constant PTSD triggers," she says. By following her parents' definition of "love your neighbor," by sitting around and taking their sins without offering them any consequences, Patricia admits, "I was, quite literally, killing myself."

Eventually, through prayer and counseling, Patricia has been able to see their sin for what it was and lift that responsibility off of her shoulders and place it back where it belonged: on her parents. She took responsibility for her own choices so that she could be free to love in truth both her family of origin and her own husband and children. All of us with parents who demand we stay enmeshed with them must set apart those things for which we are responsible from those things over which we have no responsibility, no matter what the people from our past try to tell us. Jesus wants us to live in him, which means he wants us to live in truth, and the truth will set us free.

The simplest way I've found for establishing the truth in my relationships, whether it be with my family of origin, my own children, or that truck driver who nearly ran me off the road, is to take a piece of paper and write down every single fact I can about whatever conflict is currently upsetting me, draining my energy, and taking my focus off of what God wants me to do. Next, I take another piece of paper and draw a line down the middle of it. On the left, I copy down all the facts that fall under my responsibility. On the right, I write down all the facts that are not my responsibility. For example, when one of my very young children is fighting against learning the discipline of prayer time, the facts fall this way:

My Responsibility	Not My Responsibility
• Teach my kids prayer	• Child's resistance to prayer
• Teach my kids patience	
	• Child's tears
• Teach self-control	• Child's pouting
• Teach that choices have consequences	• Child's present lack of patience
• The words I say	• Child's obedience
• My feelings of frustration at having a child who doesn't intrinsically want to honor the God who has helped me so much	• Child's feelings of frustration at having to stop whatever enjoyable activity she was doing in order to sit still

The facts on the left point out to me that, just like you can lead a horse to water but you can't make it drink, I can teach my child how to pray, but I can't actually make her pray. I also can only teach patience and self-control, but I can't make her learn it. Therefore, if she chooses to put up a stink when it's time for family rosary, then she chooses to lose privileges (in this child's case, the coveted screen time). However, her choices are out of my control, and there's no scaring loving obedience into her. In fact, resorting to violence (verbal or otherwise) is not teaching patience or self-control, and to do so would not be an honest acceptance of my responsibilities as a parent. I can't make *her* pray, but *she* can't make me give her the iPad. Whether or not I teach her to pray and be virtuous is between me and God. Whether or not she accepts those lessons is between her and God.

Of course, we always need to balance all truths against each other. As a parent tasked with the job of teaching God's children how to find and follow him, I have a right to withhold a luxury item like screen time. I never have a right to withhold necessities like safety, food, clothing, shelter, or affection. Are you having trouble figuring out how to discipline your children and still love them as the little neighbors that they are? Jesus offers us a bit of a self-check in what might seem like an unlikely Scripture: Mark 2:23–28. In this scene, the Pharisees are complaining about how Jesus is letting his disciples pick grain on the Sabbath. Jesus points out, "The sabbath was made for man, not man for the sabbath." In the same way, discipline is made for children, not children for discipline. Ask yourself, in truth, are you disciplining your kids for their own growth or to keep them from making you feel something uncomfortable, like frustration, helplessness, or loneliness?

The more we practice differentiating responsibilities, the more naturally healthy boundaries will come to us. There will be more on boundaries in the chapter on meekness, but for now, for a first step, ask God to give you the courage to set good boundaries as he did and still does in his relationship with all of us, his children.

Good fences make good neighbors, and that little responsibility table exercise offered above is one practice you can use in mending the fences between you and your neighbor, one of the tools you can use to parent better than you yourself were parented. Do you want to fulfill God's command to love these people in your life? Then don't focus on getting them to do what you want them to do. Focus on getting yourself to do what God wants you to do. That's truth, which means that's love. With any luck — no, with any *mercy* — they'll take the hint and jump on that train, and they'll start putting their own chunky necklaces on their own individual hooks.

But we are talking about free creatures with independent wills.

What if they don't? And when they don't, how do we maintain the compassion and the joy that God intends for us?

Getting a Parenting Attune-up

> He said to his disciples, "Things that cause sin will inev-
> itably occur, but woe to the person through whom they
> occur. It would be better for him if a millstone were put
> around his neck and he be thrown into the sea than for
> him to cause one of these little ones to sin. Be on your
> guard! If your brother sins, rebuke him; and if he repents,
> forgive him. And if he wrongs you seven times in one day
> and returns to you seven times saying, 'I am sorry,' you
> should forgive him." (Luke 17:1–4)

If you grew up in an enmeshed family, chances are you have a bruised version of what forgiveness looks like. Perhaps, like Patricia, you were taught that your parents could do no wrong and therefore needed no forgiveness, and that to point out their sin was a violation of the commandment "Honor your father and mother." Or maybe you grew up hearing "I'm sorry, but … " by which you were taught that it was your filial duty to excuse a parent's every sin and sweep it under the rug. Then again, perhaps the Scripture quoted above, about forgiving repeatedly, was fed to you with a dose of poison, convincing you that an apology was all that was needed to heal a relationship and rebuild broken trust, that actual penitential amends were superfluous.

Bringing these messages into your own parenting journey is a surefire way to kill any compassion you can develop for your children, for yourself, and even your unrepentant family of origin (and they need real compassion, too, even if they're still demanding appeasement). Those messages still can sneak into our best efforts, though. I know they did for me and sometimes still do. I came into parenting, guns blazing, all fired up to break the cycle and not make any of those mistakes that my parents made, by golly! And then when I made similar mistakes, all new mistakes, or any kind of mistake at all, I got trapped in my own shame. I'd only proven myself a failure, hadn't I? As a result of such thinking, too often I disconnected emotionally from my children exactly when they needed me most — to show them the example of humble compassion that they need to learn in order to build relationships. The perfection my parents expected of me became the perfection I expected of myself as a parent, and when my kids messed up, I took that to mean that I'd messed up, and it just got joylessly ugly from there.

It doesn't have to stay joyless. When we develop compassion and model it for our children, we participate in the healing cycle that God built into us as a sort of fail-safe in the face of the Fall. One term for this is the "rupture/repair" cycle.

If you put them on a scale, there are quite literally at least a ton of books available that talk about emotional connection in parenting. However, if you're searching for a single resource that provides both information and exercises for self-connection that translate into a number of healthy parenting skills, take a look at Aundi Kolber's *Try Softer: A Fresh Approach to Move Us Out of Anxiety, Stress, and Survival Mode — and Into a Life of Connection and Joy.* Yes, it's a long title, but it provides a useful introduction in the neuroscience of how we feel the things we feel and practices we can adopt to help us have richer relationships.

Regarding the rupture/repair cycle, Kolber synthesizes decades of parenting science to show us that we don't have to be perfect; we just have to be compassionate. First, she describes that a parent needs to develop skills in *attunement,* which is responsiveness to the needs of another. In parenting, this means responsiveness to the needs of the child. However, she writes, "Even the most loving parents don't respond to their children perfectly, which is why the concept of repair is vital. A repair occurs when caregivers recognize they've misattuned to their children and then figure out a way to reconnect, apologize, or take whatever step is needed."

She goes on to describe a situation where a mother loses her patience with a child who is having a difficult time controlling his tendency to interrupt. The mother's impatience is an example of misattunement that causes a rupture: She reacted to her son as if he was intentionally driving her crazy, but in truth, his interruptions were simply his age-appropriate way of trying to get his needs met. The mother in this situation then initiates a repair by first reattuning to her son: She is attentive to the fact that her response caused him pain and disconnection. Then she apologizes, telling her son how his interruptions made her feel frustrated, but then admitting that her response was not right, no matter how frustrated she was. Kolber then writes, "As the mom repairs the gap she created with her son, she becomes reattuned to his experience, and the son will move through the moment, confident once again in the security of his mom."[14]

Once that security is reestablished, the parent has the credibility to correct her son's interrupting habit compassionately. By showing her son that she's there for him even in both of their mistakes, the mother guides their relationship through the rupture/repair cycle, thus strengthening their bond to withstand the inevitable future ruptures.

There will be more on attunement and reattunement in Chapter Four, when we talk about emotions as assets rather than liabilities. No matter how dedicated we are to being cycle-breakers, we are fallen creatures taught by fallen creatures. We will experience ruptures with our own children — who also happen to be fallen creatures. In fact, if we look at all of salvation history through the lens of attunement and compassion, we see that God gave us

---

14. Aundi Kolber, *Try Softer: A Fresh Approach to Move Us Out of Anxiety, Stress, and Survival Mode — and Into a Life of Connection and Joy* (Carol Stream, IL: Tyndale Momentum, 2020), 85–86.

the rupture/repair cycle in response to our fallenness. When we turned from our own needs to be connected with God, sin introduced misattunement. Thankfully, God will never let himself be outdone by our sin. He didn't just pursue humanity in law and prophets throughout the Old Testament. He *became* attunement when he took on our flesh. He took our rejection even to the point of a brutal death. Then, rather than throwing that brutality back at us, he accepted our desires as they were. He was freed for eternity through the resurrection to show us that nobody's sins, not our parents' and not even our children's, can destroy us, if only we'll attune to his good desires for us.

That last bit bears repeating: *Attune to his good desires for us.* This is important enough to repeat because of the harsh reality of life in a fallen world. We know our parents are fallen creatures. God willing, we see our own failings. Our children, depending on their developmental levels in the present moment, may be innocent or not, but they are also fallen creatures. We need to accept that, even if we initiate the repair phase of rupture/repair, our attunement and repairs might not be received as we'd hoped. Please don't be shocked, as I have been, that even doing everything "right" to repair everything I'd just done wrong — in other words, when checking off all the boxes of compassion and reattunement in repairing matters with your sinned-against kids — those repairs seem unreceived. Sometimes reattuning to my kids has just given them the message that it's safe with Mommy, and, often enough, my kids take that safety as a place to keep venting anger against me because they now know they won't be punished for their feelings. Sometimes they know that it's safe to hurt me back, so they do the thing they know hurts me the most: ignore me.

Not gonna lie, my fellow cycle-breakers. It's hard to stay attuned through that. So hard. I mean, didn't I just do what is supposed to make things better? Why do I feel so much worse? Then again, how often do I do the same to God? How often do I just keep raging at him or ignoring him after he's given me mercy, poured love onto me through Scripture and the sacraments, reached out to me through friends who remind me of my worth through those precious but admittedly less intense relationships than my family provides?

Rupture/repair and reattunement are difficult because they are the cross. They are the moments that image the whole of salvation history in the countless shouts, tears, sighs, and hugs that pass between family members. Paul even writes about how we can trust God to be attuned to us, his children, through the rupture and repair cycle in Hebrews 4:15–16, which reads: "For we do not have a high priest who is unable to sympathize with our weaknesses, but one who has similarly been tested in every way, yet without sin. So let us confidently approach the throne of grace to receive mercy and to find grace for timely help."

Remember how I said that, when confronting family sins, you're not standing up *to* your family but *for* Christ? Well, when you participate in the rupture/repair cycle, you're not humbling yourself *to* your family but *to* Christ. Jesus wants us to love as he did, compassionately. If we really want to break the cycle of family abuse and dysfunction, we must embrace the ruptures not as failures of our parents, ourselves, or our children to listen, but as opportunities for repair. Thus we are freed to live love of neighbor and self through compassion with ourselves and our children. We must embrace the cross in all our relationships. That is how we exchange frustration and resentment for peace and joy. That is how we will embrace eternal life.

The F-Word
All of that said, I know from personal experience how difficult it can be to establish compassion through rupture/repair, since I experienced so little of it myself in my formative years and, to be frank, still don't experience it with my children's grandparents.

How do we carry compassion into our parenting lives, showering forgiveness and attunement on our own children, when we carry so many wounds and may experience so many violated boundaries with our own parents, even after we've left their nests? God has given us the authority to participate in relationship repair with our children, especially in the years before they become independent adults, but how do we repair a relationship with our own parents, persons over whom we have no authority, persons who are very likely to rebel at any suggestion that they might have something to repair?

In other words, how do we forgive people who remain convinced that they don't need forgiveness? We cycle-breakers owe it to ourselves and our relationships with our children to embrace the cross that remains present in a relationship with a parent or parents who refuse their crosses, often trying to make us carry them instead.

God created a world where we have free will, and we can use that free will to sin. But no sin is without its eventual consequence. Every sin causes a rupture in the sinner's relationship with all of humanity, but especially with those people closest to him. Any time a sinner tries using Scripture or Church teaching to avoid the consequences of sin, it's just like that breezy time of day in the Garden of Eden with our first parents. God knows where we are. He gives us a chance to admit it, but if we don't, we still lose paradise. Any parent who tries convincing a child otherwise for the sake of her own ego is compounding sin upon sin, violating that child's unique boundaries, and throwing up a wall between parent and child that only God can break down — and, as we've already seen, God is King of Boundaries. He won't violate our free will by making us do something we don't want to do. He won't make your sinful parents apologize to you and mean it. Compassion is a choice. They have to desire of their own accord to restore your relationship. God wants us to both forgive and honor our parents, but it's vital to our own holiness that we learn that forgiveness is not the same thing as reconciliation, and honor is not a rug under which we are to sweep anyone's failings.

Do you remember a few pages back where I rattled off a list of all the instances where Jesus told people that their sins were forgiven? In every single one of those situations, the people forgiven, when confronted with their need for forgiveness, surrendered to Jesus. They just stood there and let Jesus forgive them. This was in complete contrast to what the Pharisees did in general, but especially in the story of the man born blind. The Pharisees committed the same sins-upon-sins that mentally unhealthy, spiritually unholy parents (and people in general) tend to do:

- **Blame-shifting**: The Pharisees accused Jesus of breaking the Sabbath. How have your parents blamed you for their sins?
- **Devaluing**: The Pharisees discounted the experience of the healed person when they said, "You were born totally in sin, and are you trying to teach us?" How have your parents minimized your hurt and accusations in order to brush off the pain of having hurt their own children?
- **Denial**: Have your parents, like the Pharisees in the face of their accusers, cried out, "Surely we are not also blind, are we?"

So how do we forgive people who remain convinced that they don't need forgiveness? How can God renew a relationship like this? As always, Jesus leads the way. Parents aren't entitled to do what they want just because they're in charge of weaker, dependent people. All authority is from God (see Romans 13). That doesn't guarantee that sinful humans will use authority in a godly way. Church teaching goes on to confirm this. The *Catechism* states that the family is called to be a place where the parents and children connect emotionally and affectionately through shared respect. Here the Church calls the family "a privileged community" where honor for God and morality are fostered. The Church, however, like any good and holy mother, knows her children are imperfect. The *Catechism* acknowledges this reality by stating, "The family should live in such a way that its members learn to care and take responsibility for the young, the old, the sick, the handicapped, and the poor. There are many families who are at times incapable of providing this help." Further on, the Church clearly states that children owe their parents obedience *except when the parents are asking for obedience in sin*. When our parents chose to lead by examples not worth following, they didn't just betray us, their children. They also betrayed God's loving design. They continue to do so when, in their denial, they remain unrepentant (cf. CCC 2206–08, 2217).

So if God commands us to honor these parents, and he also commands us to obey him in all things (read: live up to reality), then how are we supposed to honor these people he chose for us knowing full well they'd be unrepentant — at least so far? It is no honor to your parents to pretend they're perfect and thus appease sinful expectations. What we can do, regardless of whether or not our parents have made themselves safe people in the here and now, is honor the fact that our parents did for us something that no one else in the history of humanity could have done: given us life. The circumstances of our conception don't matter. The mental health, holiness, or lack thereof are irrelevant to the fact — the reality, the *truth* — that these people, sinners like the rest of us, had a part in your existence and your opportunity to know and love the God who will always love us better than even the most perfect parent ever could. You can honor your parents without their repentance, even without ever speaking to them again. While going no-contact shouldn't be the first option for dealing with unrepentant parents, sometimes it is the only practicable option that limits their opportunity to sin against you and your children and thus dig their own holes deeper and deeper, all the way to hell if they wish. You honor your parents when you pray for them to be healed of their blindness so that they can hear those precious words of God's forgiveness.

Forgiving them on earth does not have to be reconciliation either. Reconciliation requires that the injurer accepts responsibility and makes efforts to set things right on the injured party's terms. Reconciliation requires compassionate rupture/ repair. You may never get that from your parents. You're not alone, though: Jesus may never get reconciliation from them either. Forgiveness, however, is a different creature. At the Last Supper, Jesus made it clear that forgiveness requires nothing of the sinner. This is made clear when, in Matthew 26:28, he calls the cup of his blood, "my blood of the covenant, which will be shed on behalf of many for the forgiveness of sins." He doesn't say that his blood is only for the people who are nice to him. His blood is for the forgiveness of sins. He gives it freely. It is our choice whether or not to accept this generous gift, which only those "many" (not all) who seek union with him will receive.

Forgiveness simply means accepting that you had no hand in others' sins against you. You honor the boundary between yourself and, in the case of family abuse, the parent who abused you, when you surrender others' sins and stop trying to drag anyone's unwilling behind into heaven. Surrender lets Jesus purify them — and us — far better than we ever could, frail and fallen humans that we are. And if they rebel at the idea of being purified? Whenever Jesus casts out demons, those demons and their hosts get angry. They fight against anything good. Let Jesus cast that out of *you*, but don't be surprised when others don't want that cast out of themselves.

Unlearning What We Lived

Pope Saint John Paul II said, "To maintain a joyful family requires much from both the parents and the children. Each member of the family has to become, in a special way, the servant of the others."[15] It is a bitter thing, recognizing that your parents weren't as loving as they were called to be. However, there is a sweetness, too. You already know how *not* to love your neighbor. Your soul is sensitive to sin because you recognize that someone who was supposed to love you failed. Your road has guardrails. You still need the rest of the rules of the road — the rest of the boundaries. When we pursue truth in holiness, the boundaries pretty much show themselves. This pursuit of holiness is important because, unless we are confident about the rightness or wrongness of parenting choices in and of themselves — independent of whether or not we chose them or others chose to parent us with them — we will be standing on shaky ground with our own children. We run the risk of clouding our consciences with enmeshment. We run the risk of finding poison in the parenting pantry and using it, unwittingly or with a conscious denial of conscience, on our own children. We run the risk of selling our joy for the cost of appeasement.

I assume you don't want to do that. You wouldn't be dropping good money on a book that's about breaking the cycle of family dysfunction if you didn't already recognize that you did, in fact, grow up in a dysfunctional family. You're reading this because you're on Team Break the Cycle. There are all kinds of betrayal that put you on that team. The worst, perhaps, or at least deepest, is the fact that God designed us to learn from our parents. Do you know what this means? This means God, the Creator of the universe, the Supreme Being, the Uncaused Cause, the comforter of all our afflictions, is *on your side*. He's rooting for you. The Trin-

---

15. John Paul II, "Apostolic Journey to the United States of America, Holy Mass at the Capital Mall, Washington (homily)," October 7, 1979 (Vatican: Libreria Editrice Vaticana), par. 5.

ity is up there on the heavenly bleachers wearing matching Team Break the Cycle T-shirts. Now, that doesn't mean that God is rooting against your parents, but more on that in a bit. It *does* mean that God is cheering for you to model your family after his good and generous plan. So take heart. You've already got the biggest cheering section there is in your fight to become a loving parent.

This is what a Christian family is called to be, then: a place where here on earth we can eat the food of a heavenly life. Love is the main course made up of simple, quality ingredients — ingredients Jesus handed even the most wounded of us when he gave us the Sermon on the Mount. We commonly call these ingredients for living a holy, healthy, affectionate life the Beatitudes. The Beatitudes offer soul medicine, healing the hurts we brought with us so that we can love our neighbors — our parents, children, and even that truck driver — compassionately in the here and now for the sake of the eternal. As we sort together through our pile of mixed-up scarves and necklaces, we will look at each of these Beatitudes in turn in the coming chapters.

HOLY FAMILY MOMENT
Saint Joseph Takes Mary into His Home (Mt 1:18–25)

By all appearances, Joseph had been cheated on, shamed before the entire town of Nazareth, not to mention anyone in the hill country of Judah who'd seen Mary on her journey to and from Elizabeth's house. By anyone's standards — heck, by Moses' standards — Joseph was within his rights to have Mary stoned to death for betraying him. Already, however, even before the angel appears to him, we see in Saint Joseph a love of neighbor, even when that neighbor appears to be an enemy.

Jesus knows that our families are our closest neighbors, and that they have great capacity to hurt us. He gives us the example of his foster father to show us that, when we put mercy first, especially when we are betrayed, he will lead us into miracles. After all, the God who can bring about a virgin birth can certainly help you be a righteous man (or woman) after the model of Saint Joseph. Joseph chose compassion over fear, letting God lead him and his family through many snares into their eternal destiny.

BEATITUDE BASIC WORKSHOP
Compassion

1. Having a conflict with a family member? Make two lists: one of all the things in the conflict that are your responsibility, another of all the things that are not your responsibility. Think about the conflict from your family member's point of view, and make choices based only on your responsibilities.

2. Ask God to show you good boundaries and to give you strength when you must point out another's sins. Remember, it is Christlike to tell others that they've sinned. It's also Christlike to let them walk away from the truth if they so choose.

3. Journal about the thought that discipline is made for children, not children for discipline. How might that inform some of your parenting choices? How might that reframe how you see your own parents' treatment of you?

PRAYER TO OBTAIN THE
CONFIDENCE OF A CHILD[16]

Mary, pray with me to obtain the gift that I may have the confi-

---

16. A. Francis Coomes, *Mother's Manual*, "For the Confidence of a Child" (Brooklyn: William J. Hirten Co. Inc., 1973), 51–52.

dence of my child [children]. As you know, a mother needs this confidence in order to guide her children properly. When there are difficulties, or problems, or troubles, may they be shared with me trustingly, that I may more readily perform a mother's task of helping her child. And, Mother most prudent, when this confidence is shown, obtain the grace that I may know how to help and instruct my child; that I may not only have the wisdom and prudence which is needed then to direct my child, but that I may also have the courage to say in a way that will be truly helpful the things children should know. Be to me a mother of good counsel and, through the grace you can bring, direct me at all times in the responsibilities of my holy office of motherhood. Amen.

Seat of Wisdom, pray for me!

SAINT-SPIRATION
Saint Catherine of Siena

Catherine of Siena shows us that one adult child striving for holiness can entice a whole family into heaven. Young Catherine promised her life to Jesus, but Catherine's mother especially was eager for Catherine to make a good earthly marriage match. Alas, Catherine did everything she could to avoid acquiring an earthly spouse. In retaliation, the large Benincasa family (two parents and twelve other children) deprived Catherine of privacy, heaping verbal abuse on her and overloading her with chores in hopes that she would change her mind. Rather than growing bitter against her family, Catherine set about serving them, imagining her father as Our Father, her mother as Our Lady, her brothers as the apostles. At last, seeing that their maltreatment of her only made her more serene, her family relented and let her live at home in peace.

As her parents aged, Catherine begged Jesus to let her father forgo purgatory. Jesus replied that this was not possible. Catherine offered to take her father's purgatory for him during her life. She immediately received a pain in her chest that she would have with her until her dying day. Later, Catherine's mother died, refusing the sacraments. Through Saint Catherine's immediate intercession, her mother revived. For the rest of her life, Catherine's mother became one of the saint's most devoted disciples, and by all reports took her second earthly death in a state of grace.

Because she never stopped seeing her family as worthy of service, Catherine led the Benincasas to heaven with her beloved Spouse.[17]

17. Jeanne Marie, "Saint Catherine of Siena," Catholicism.org, accessed February 16, 2021, http://catholicism.org/saint-catherine-of-siena.html.

— 3 —

BLESSED ARE THE POOR IN SPIRIT

For Theirs Is the Kingdom of Heaven

Beatitude Basic: Teachability

Therefore, prophesy and say to them: Thus says the Lord GOD:
Look! I am going to open your graves;
I will make you come up out of your graves, my people,
And bring you back to the land of Israel.
You shall know that I am the LORD,
When I open your graves
And make you come up out of them, my people!
I will put my spirit in you that you may come to life, and
I will settle you in your land.
Then you shall know that I am the LORD. I have spoken;
I will do it — oracle of the LORD.

— Ezekiel 37:12–14

Independent Study

I was three years into both my undergraduate degree in theatre and my awareness that the coping techniques I'd learned from my parents weren't especially healthy ones. I'd taken on three credits of independent study in directing the department's children's theatre production for the semester. I'd chosen my gentle but honest, good-humored, Minnesotan-through-and-through directing professor Dr. Ollerman as my project advisor. We were about a week and a half out from taking the show on tour to local elementary schools before opening night on campus, but the delightful script was starting to wear on the actors and me. The charm and humor just weren't coming through in rehearsals, and I couldn't figure out why not. The actors knew their lines. I'd seen all but a handful of them act before and knew their talent. The strange thing was that, in spite of all our rehearsal time, and in spite of all my suggestions that the actors try different delivery methods, none of them ever seemed to take my suggestions to heart. They just kept doing the same old thing. The show was getting stale, and we hadn't even been in front of an audience yet. I was dreading our first show.

One night, after the actors had left the rehearsal space, Dr. Ollerman kept me behind to talk about the progress he was seeing, or lack thereof. He went about it in his indirect but totally effective way.

"You've been doing a lot of run-throughs, haven't you?"

"Yeah," I admitted. "That's pretty much all we've been doing."

He nodded thoughtfully. "What do you think that might be doing towards the end result?"

I felt my shoulders tighten. I felt the words bubble up in my throat, words of self-defense, deflection, and yet more self-defense. *What do you think it's doing? I'm trying my best, aren't I? Didn't you teach me to do run-throughs until it's polished?*

Before I could even get any of those words out, Dr. Ollerman added, "Have you seen any of the actors trying anything new?"

I held all those defensive words in my mind for another moment. Could I let them go and survive being wrong? I hadn't grown up with anyone admitting they're wrong. What would happen if I did? In that moment, I somehow realized that I had a choice. I could insist on being right and keep doing things the same way I'd been doing them, or I could risk being wrong and possibly have a better show than the one we had so far.

"I haven't," I confessed, which stung my ego. I replayed his questions in my mind, and at last the lights came on in my mind. *A lot of run-throughs.* "Oh. I get it. With all these plain run-throughs, I'm just making them practice their mistakes."

Admitting this, I looked up and saw something in Dr. Ollerman's smile I'd never seen before. He was delighting in the fact that I was finding my way out of the rut into which I'd let my cast wander. He was delighting in the fact that I'd let myself be teachable. We brainstormed exercises I could do with the cast to bring them out of memorization mode and into a mindset that would make the play come alive. Okay, so the cast wasn't thrilled with me for making them rehearse their lines not with words but with animal sounds representing their characters, but we were all delighted with the result. The show was a success, on tour and on campus. Oh, and I got an A in independent study.

I've often heard that the definition of insanity is doing the same thing over and over again and expecting different results. I'm not sure how valid that is, since that could also be the definition of persistence. To this day, however, I think back to that moment with Dr. Ollerman and wonder at it. Somewhere in giving my life to Christ in my freshman year of college, Christ in turn gave me a gift that my parents wouldn't, couldn't, or simply didn't: the gift of being able to see a need for change in myself, and then the strength to make that change. I let myself be wrong. In that wrongness, I got my first taste of the gift of being teachable.

I was too new in my intentional faith walk to know that I already was experiencing the "blessed" part of "Blessed are the poor in spirit."

A New Script: The Beatitudes

Let's think back to the idea of a parenting pantry. We look at the ingredients we've been given, and we must throw them out because they are toxic: physical violence, screaming, shame, blame-shifting, neglect, dismissiveness, selfishness, control, harsh criticism. Just like the Israelites freshly out of slavery in Egypt and newly delivered of the Ten Commandments, we know the "thou shalt nots." We know what not to do. But God is a good father, and he knows that we need more than directions on the negative. He knows we need directions on what *to* do instead. That is why, in preparing to give us the new covenant of his blood on the cross, Jesus first climbed a mountain, sat his people down, and gave them directions on how to live within the boundaries of freedom. In other words, in the Sermon on the Mount, he gave us the Beatitudes. He gave us a new script.

This is a gift especially to those of us without good models in our own earthly parents. If you're not yet familiar, go read Matthew 5:1–12. Jesus tells us that in every pain we will ever encounter, we are blessed. This is so foreign to those of us who have avoided conflict so that we don't displease easily angered parents, but this is how our heavenly Father sees us. He sees every pain we've ever felt through others shaming us, blaming us, neglecting and dismissing our infinite value as precious children of God. He sees that pain and treasures it. Best of all, he never dismisses that pain. He lifted it high on the cross in his own body, thereby not just telling us but showing us, "The pain you feel from living in a sinful world is so valuable that I embraced it and turned it into eternal life. It may hurt, but as long as you are united in my love, it cannot kill you." Through resurrection joy,

Jesus doesn't obliterate our pain, but he does use it to make our whole world new.

Before the crucifixion and Resurrection even happened, Jesus got to work laying the foundation for how to follow him, even when it would be scary, even when it would hurt, even when it would look impossible and fruitless and go against everything we'd ever been taught by real humans breathing in our faces. Following him to the cross, through the cross, and into eternal life requires that we turn our backs on sin, but not just others' sins against us. We also have to defy our own bad habits and sins. We have to surrender ourselves completely to him, and in *that* we are blessed. The Beatitudes tell us how to do just that.

The Beatitudes also tell us that our struggles in doing so are precious to Jesus. They make him feel loved. They fill him with the desire to draw us closer to him so that we don't have to summon our own bravery anymore. We can just fill ourselves with his. In that perfect bravery, we are free to face all the discomfort, both spiritual and occasionally physical, that the purification process requires of us. The Book of Revelation promises us that nothing impure can enter heaven (see 21:27). Jesus makes us pure by his blood on the cross. He also gave us the Beatitudes to help us find our way to him there, to see the value in his pain and ours, to notice the blessings brought into our lives rather than to just see ourselves as perpetual victims.

In the Beatitudes, Jesus tells us that it's not that God wants us to suffer. It's just that God doesn't want us to suffer alone.

Giddyup

My oldest two daughters tried a horseback riding lesson once. They were not quite nine years old, if memory serves. We were waiting by the barn for the instructor to arrive, and while we did, we watched one of the older riders trying to bring her horse into the barn for post-ride grooming. It was a lovely spring day after a typically dreary winter, and I guess that horse did not want to trade the pleasant sun for being cleaned all over with necessary-but-irritating combs because it wasn't long before that horse was rearing up and pawing the air. The rider, an older teen who had been leading him, turned and swatted toward him with her riding crop.

"C'mon, Louie!" I remember her shouting. She then muttered, "He is just so stubborn!"

I must have been staring at this exchange with maternal terror in my eyes because in the next moment I heard the barn owner say next to me, "Don't worry, Mom. The horses we have for your girls are gentle old mares. They're much smaller. They aren't as spirited."

I probably sighed a bigger sigh of relief than my girls did! My girls moved on with this instructor, who introduced them to two short, gentle horses named Cheyenne and Teddy. As they tacked up their less-than-majestic mounts, I divided my attention between watching them work and watching the older girl still struggling to get Louie the Spirited into the barn.

A year or so later, it was time to study the Beatitudes with my kids. As I prepared, I got stuck on the very first one. What does it mean to be "poor in spirit" anyway? As a child in Catholic school, I'd always thought and been taught that it had meant being low energy, weak, compliant. That didn't quite fit, though, with reality. Should we be low energy in the face of evils like peer pressure to try illegal drugs? Should we comply with something that would hurt us? Was I, like my mother said, guilty of parent abuse because I told her to stop touching me where she had no place to touch? Was self-defense a vice and not a virtue?

As I then prepared to talk Beatitudes with my kids, I came across author Charles Latham's writing on being poor in spirit … and Westerns? Yep, he contrasted the wild horses he'd seen on old cowboy movies with the gentle, tourist-grade trail horses he'd ridden in real life.[18] I then thought about the difference between the mellow mares my kids had met and ridden at the barn versus Louie, rearing up against the leading of his older, more experienced rider. Not much later, I came across Psalm 32:

> I will instruct you and show you the way you should walk,
> give you counsel with my eye upon you.
> Do not be like a horse or mule, without understanding;
> with bit and bridle their temper is curbed,
> else they will not come to you. (Psalm 32:8–9)

This combination of prayer, reading, and experience completely opened my eyes to what it really means to be poor in spirit. Being poor in spirit does not mean being a doormat or letting people sin against you repeatedly with no consequences. It means to accept teaching, to be willing to be wrong and admit it. A person who is poor in spirit accepts correction graciously, even if it comes from those of perceived lower status than themselves. It means no longer fighting against the call to repent and change direction, but to change one's behaviors so that one can connect more closely with others. It means being tame enough that even clumsy, anxious, untrained children can be trusted with you, and you will not hurt them.

You wouldn't be reading this book if your parents had been truly poor in spirit.

Maybe Cheyenne and Teddy had been born with milder temperaments than Louie, but I'm willing to bet that somewhere along the way even Cheyenne and Teddy had to be trained in gentleness in order to let children ride them. We fallen humans have a huge advantage over horses. We can choose that training ourselves. We can learn how to be less spirited and more docile for our children,

---

18 Charles Latham, *Step by Step: Looking at the New Testament Beatitudes Through the Old Testament Feasts* (Spring Hill, TN: Holy Fire Publishing, 2005), 53.

who need our gentleness, but also to our God, who craves our closeness. Yes, God who created us craves our closeness. You may think you want God in your life, but that desire is just a shadow of his desire for you.

Once we let go of our spiritedness, our resistance to teaching, correction, and change, we free ourselves to follow Jesus into the very depths of his unconditional love for us. Once we practice docility, we will stop fighting against the ways in which God chooses to teach us, most frequently through denying us what we think we want. We'll be free to stop screaming any time an immature person (child or parent) screams at us. We will be free to go where God leads and thus learn what is important to him. We will begin to see how we might win hearts rather than control others' actions. We will have made ourselves so poor in our own spirit that we will suddenly have room to be made rich in God's spirit of love, justice, mercy, and healing.

Bit and Bridle or Riding Crop?

What makes wrongly-spirited humans so bad at parenting is that they're trying to convince themselves and all future generations of an outright lie: that they're never wrong and have nothing to learn. God's not buying that lie, but like our shared ancestor, World's First Murderer Cain, they kind of don't care, nor have they figured out that maybe they should. Spirited humans buy the lie that they can never be wrong and weakness is intolerable. Is it any wonder that parents who do not cultivate poverty of spirit shut their children out and down through abusive and dysfunctional patterns? They aren't willing to be wrong, to change, and to become more like Christ, who is all that is truly right. God warns us against being this kind of unteachable.

- If we say, "We are without sin," we deceive ourselves, and the truth is not in us. If we acknowledge

our sins, he is faithful and just and will forgive our
sins and cleanse us from every wrongdoing. If we
say, "We have not sinned," we make him a liar, and
his word is not in us. (see 1 Jn 1:8–10)
- As dogs return to their vomit, so fools repeat
  their folly. (Prv 26:11)
- For godly sorrow produces a salutary repentance
  without regret, but worldly sorrow produces
  death. (2 Cor 7:10)

In fact, there's even a chunk of Proverbs 9 dedicated to teaching us how to identify a wise person:

Whoever corrects the arrogant earns insults;
    and whoever reproves the wicked incurs opprobrium.
Do not reprove the arrogant, lest they hate you;
    reprove the wise, and they will love you.
Instruct the wise, and they become still wiser;
    teach the just, and they advance in learning.
                            (Proverbs 9:7–9)

The wise person wants to learn. Wickedness is equivalent with not wanting to learn and getting angry at anyone who asks you to. So what do you do if you were taught wickedness and not wisdom?

I like to think about the human family as being a grown-up factory: The family is designed to produce and launch not perpetual children but actual grown-ups. Just like other factories, some of these grown-up factories are awesome and launch grown-ups that come with highly functional factory settings: They know how to speak truth, expect truth from others, and they know how to admit when they're wrong and how to forgive when others have been wrong. Some factories, however, are just low quality. The grown-ups they launch have factory settings that don't function well and only perpetuate falsehood in relationships: 0/5, would not recommend. We all deserve to come out of an awesome factory, but it's not our fault if we didn't.

Here's the awesome thing about being a human: No matter what default settings we brought with us into adulthood, God knitted us together in our mother's wombs well before we were placed in that grown-up factory — our families of origin. As raw products, God has created us to be infinitely customizable. All factory products come out with default settings, but the end-user can customize and optimize for better performance. My family of origin may have set my default to "I must be perfect, or no one will love me." Unfortunately, this means I default to wickedness in one way or another. I'll be some kind of a perfectionist, and when I make my inevitable mistakes and sins, I'll crumble at my failings, or I'll be so afraid of my own mistakes that I'll spend my energy convincing myself and those I hurt most (usually those I love the most — my spouse and children) that I don't make mistakes, and they're the ones mistaken for ever suggesting that I could. These approaches are, as God tells us above, foolish, wicked, and only lead to death. Death can take many forms: of heart, of soul, of identity, of relationship, and of ability to form new and healthy relationships. Death here can even mean death of the body, for how many children lose their lives one way or another to a parent's physical abuse?

Holding on to our delusions about our own perfection — in other words, being spirited — hurts the people we love, but it does us no favors either. Thus it should come as no surprise that we need to reconfigure our defaults and set up a new custom parenting behavior profile. No, it's not fair that we have to do this. However, it is something we can do while telling Jesus, "I should not have to do this, but you should not have had to die on the cross. I will take this task up in penance for the sins of my parents who shaped me this way, just as you took up your cross in penance for the sins of humanity who shaped our world into a badly broken one in need of salvation."

Of course, it feels bad to admit that we've hurt people and have work to do. However, if we cling to the lie that we are already perfect, we're already working too hard, pouring energy into unreality. People can't trust us because it's obvious to everyone but us that we are living a lie. So if we want to get rid of that lie and bring reality back into our hearts, first we're going to have to face feeling bad. It feels bad to hurt people. It's supposed to. But the more we run from that pain, the farther we run from the people who love us and need us. If we never face those bad feelings that come when we acknowledge that we've hurt someone, we can never feel forgiveness, which means we can never feel secure or connected to anyone we've hurt. We deprive ourselves and others of the joy borne of the rupture/repair cycle. We, like our equine friend Louie, are fighting so hard against going home to receive care we cannot provide for ourselves. The spirited know no rest.

Jesus knew what he was doing when he first described the poor in spirit as blessed. Being teachable is equivalent to being just because justice is harmony with reality, with truth. Not having to fight day and night against reality brings the greatest peace available this side of earth. That's the definition of "blessed."

The Teachable Teacher

So we know that when we make ourselves poor in spirit, when we let go of our spiritedness and stop fighting reality, when we make ourselves teachable, we connect in a very real way with truth. In John 14:6, Jesus tells us he is the truth. Therefore, being teachable connects us directly to the heart of Jesus in spite of our failings. Of course, poverty of spirit is hard enough to cultivate as an independent adult. What happens when you throw children into the mix, with their tantrums, their sullenness, their impulsivity and reluctance to follow anybody's rules, including their own? The challenge for us as parents, ourselves raised by wrongly-spirited people, is to remain poor in spirit while teaching our children, also fallen humans, how to connect with Jesus who is truth. We must tame their spirits to his loving hand without, frankly, losing our minds in the process.

When God chose us for this parenting gig, he called us to lead these children toward maturity, which, if you think of it, is just another word for poverty of spirit: the awareness that we can't always be right and that we still have much to learn. He called us to help build grown-ups. We must teach by example how to be docile, but we also must not reward them or placate them when they resist reasonable limits. Proverbs 19:18 says, "Discipline your son, for there is hope; but do not be intent on his death." The temptation as a parent to control our children through our rage can be strong, but so can the fear of providing our children with any discipline at all, lest we become like our own raging parents. I've certainly fallen into both traps many a time.

This is where our own poverty of spirit, our own teachability, can lift us up to become our children's best earthly teachers. Through our own parents' sin, our sense of a parent's duty to correct has been injured. In Matthew 7:1–5 we first are told, "Stop judging, that you may not be judged." At first glance, we may think this verse prevents us from correcting our children at all. We must read further.

> For as you judge, so will you be judged, and the measure
> with which you measure will be measured out to you.
> Why do you notice the splinter in your brother's eye, but
> do not perceive the wooden beam in your own eye?
> How can you say to your brother, 'Let me remove that
> splinter from your eye,' while the wooden beam is in
> your eye? You hypocrite, remove the wooden beam from
> your eye first; then you will see clearly to remove the

splinter from your brother's eye.

Jesus doesn't say that we are never to point out any person's sins. He just lays the rules for seeing clearly: Look to your own sins first and practice compassion, which you can only do if you are teachable, *then* you can teach others. We need to teach our children to be teachable themselves, but we must teach them with good example and consistency, not rage, verbal or physical, and not with fear-motivated neglect or permissiveness. To build a joyful family, we ourselves must model asking for help, saying sorry, repenting, and growing spiritually. In other words, we model maturity. We model being poor in spirit.

Being teachable in the face of your parents, themselves demonstrably spirited? That, of course, is another story.

The Barn You Left Behind

Sonja Corbitt is a convert to Catholicism from evangelical Protestantism. In her writing and speaking, she also relates how she's also a survivor of a very tumultuous relationship with her father, a domineering man known for controlling his relationships with fury, harshness, and inflexibility. She tells a story about how, when she was an adult, she and her father had a major blowout over his demand that she reschedule her wedding date to suit his preferences. As an adult outside of that relationship, I can see easily that such a request from a parent over an adult child is a huge overstep. Even at the time, Sonja herself could see it too. However, what she could also see was that, while her father overstepped, she also had let loose her own rage at him and his controlling behavior. In her maturity, she could see that it wasn't just *his* blowup, it was *their* blowup. She had a part to own too.

She knew God was leading her to call her father back and apologize for her part. She gathered her courage and did so. "Dad, I'm sorry for the way I treated you on that last conversation that we had." He, for his part, did not soften his heart. He did not let her apology teach him gentleness or docility. He berated her for victimizing him, but did not admit any of his own wrongdoing.

How did Sonja respond? "I didn't feel a thing. It wasn't hurtful. I wasn't angry at him. There was no emotion related to that at all, except relief and freedom! I did what God asked me to do, and he did a miracle: I threw myself up on that altar and let my dad do what he always did, but you know what? The fire did not affect me."[19] She now could withstand her father's rejection, his denial of his part in wounding her, with joy because she was able to see truth clearly in her own teachability.

This is the blessing that comes specifically to adult children of abusive and dysfunctional families who dedicate themselves not to changing their parents, not to changing a past that is past the point of change, but to learning how to be what Jesus calls them to be in the here, the now, and the future. Poverty of spirit tells us to make ourselves teachable but to let go of the teachability of others who are not under our authority. Yes, our children have been placed under our authority, and we are called to teach them as Jesus teaches us, by gentle acceptance, consistent example, and humility — which for fallen humans is the humility to admit the truth when we've sinned. Our parents, however, are not under our authority and never have been. We have neither duty nor capacity to make them teachable. In making ourselves teachable even to them, we leave behind any poison their behaviors brought to our lives because now we are nourished by truth, by Christ himself, by all that is loving and good and eternal. Their fire can no longer touch us because we are already surrounded by the fire of Christ's indomitable love.

Breaking to Harness

How did Sonja and others get to this place? This place of freedom,

---

19. Sonja Corbitt, "Healing the Father Wound," recorded talk at the 2014 Diocese of Venice, Florida, Women's Conference, https://vimeo.com/89403016.

of courage in the face of other's bucking and pawing at the air, resisting any efforts to make them safe to be around? God is a gentleman. He won't take anything we don't offer him freely. Should we find ourselves still very spirited, resisting any suggestion that we might have something to learn, God will not take that spirit away from us. He will leave us alone, untaught, untrained, and ungentled because in our pride we push him away. We will be unsafe to the helpless people entrusted to our care. We will risk being hurt by those who are even angrier and more unteachable than we are, who fight harder than we do against any correction.

Poverty of spirit doesn't cultivate itself. The best way we can make room for teachability in our lives is to quiet our minds and hearts. We do this through prayer. Even if our first prayers are selfish and hard-headed, they are a start. It is in prayer that we first have that space in which we can acknowledge that we do not have all the answers. By bringing our honesty to Jesus, he will bring his truth to life in us, not just in our thoughts but in our actions. We also dispose ourselves to hear the training voice of God when we dedicate time to reading his word in the Bible. Just as a horse trainer takes the spirited horse out daily to earn its trust and show it the good that comes to it from that training, when we make Scripture study a regular discipline with assigned times and objectives, we walk with Jesus. He becomes our trainer.

The sacraments further break the hard spirit and bend it to the gentleness and humility of Christ. In the sacraments, we submit ourselves to the channels Jesus gave us through the Church. We become docile enough, bit by bit, to receive more than just an idea of love. Sacraments provide God's tangible love. There is no cure for intractability like the Sacrament of Penance. If you look in the Bible, the only time sins are forgiven is when Jesus is present. Jesus also promises us that where two or three are gathered in his name, he is there with us (see Mt 18:20). So if Jesus alone can forgive sins, and he must be present to forgive them, then just thinking about our sins isn't enough. We were made to hear God's word of forgiveness with our ears, not just our ephemeral imaginations. There are also specific people he has asked to be that voice not of human forgiveness but of divine forgiveness; these people are priests, trained and ordained to be Christ's ears and lips (Jn 20:23). Humbling ourselves before another human but in the safety of a confessional is a natural and yet supernatural remedy for the hardness of the spirited heart. If you feel yourself resisting this, please take a look at your own spiritedness and ask yourself, "What am I afraid of? What does Jesus want to teach me? How does he want to train me, and what grace does he desire to give me through his sacraments?"

A life steeped in prayer, spiritual reading, and the sacraments cultivates poverty of spirit. Without this Beatitude working in our lives, the blessings Jesus desires to give us remain out of reach. We cannot be taught unless we are willing to learn. Unless we are first willing to learn, we cannot make sense of those pains we must mourn. We cannot become meek because we will resist meekness. We cannot seek justice rightly or reach others through mercy. We cannot know what it means to be pure in heart. We won't recognize peace even if it comes up and bites us on the nose, and we won't be persecuted for righteousness because we'll be too busy persecuting others. We will become — or remain — the abusers that our parents were.

If we do not do everything within our power to become teachable, we stand to lose the kingdom of heaven. In other words, we stand to lose everything.

The Kingdom of Heaven Is Like unto a Barn

I'm no horse whisperer, but if I had to guess, I'd say that Louie didn't want to go into the barn because he didn't trust his leader. He only trusted his momentary desires and his fears of the currycomb. Cheyenne and Teddy, however, trusted their leader to bring them through work into a place of rest. Because they had learned trust, they learned how to be trusted. To trust someone effectively means to let someone influence you. When we allow ourselves to drop our defenses and instead adopt the gentleness that belongs to the poor in spirit, we let God influence us, not our destructive, dysfunctional parents. We are made truly free. Like Teddy and Cheyenne at the end of my daughters' riding lesson, we can come home, be fed, and rest in safety, cared for and loved. That rest, that peace gained by being ruled by God and not by our fear of being wrong — that is the kingdom of heaven.

In acknowledging that we can be wrong and often are, we free ourselves to receive the joy that comes to a family that grows ever closer to what is true. However, when a horse is taught to trust humans, it's not called "taming." It's called "breaking." The horse must give up its control and submit to the influence of a person who is able to give greater safety, care, and nourishment than the horse could gain on its own — but the horse still has to surrender. If our spirits are keeping us from what is best, then our spirits, too, must be broken — broken by a loving hand, but still broken. We will have to let go of what we thought was right but turned out only to be a counterfeit.

Along the way, we will come to see more and more how our own parents failed us, and how we failed our children. It will hurt. We will have much to mourn, but the soul that resists trust cannot be comforted, cannot experience joy, cannot be made new. That's why Jesus blessed the poor in spirit first. All the other blessings, especially comfort for our mourning, only come to the teachable.

HOLY FAMILY MOMENT
The Wedding Feast at Cana (Jn 2:1–12)
"They have no more wine."

Back in my youth ministry days, a wise religious sister taught me how to deal with fractious teens. "Just do what Mary did at

Cana. Define the problem and let them own it from there." Today I like to call that "The Parenting at Cana." Mary, showing us poverty of spirit, defined the problem and left it in God's hands. She waited to see what she could be taught. And boy, did God ever deliver.

How often do we see a problem and automatically jump to a solution, either with our families of origin or with our spouses and children? We think we know all the answers, and then we kick and fight and mope when our answers aren't wanted, don't help, and otherwise damage the heart of our relationships.

Mary shows us how to bring poverty of spirit into active love toward our family members. And when Mary is interceding for us, the new wine is much better than the old.

BEATITUDE BASIC WORKSHOP
Teachability

1. Examine your conscience frequently and make both apologies and penitential amends as soon as you can manage. Frequent the sacraments, especially the Sacrament of Penance. There is no point hiding from what you need to learn.

2. Find a qualified, caring mental health practitioner who can guide you through all the places in your heart and life where you can become more teachable. See the resources listed in the back of this book for suggestions on where to find one.

3. Add a bit of fun to your practice of poverty of spirit: Pick a new skill to learn with your children. Even better, ask your child to teach you something. Whenever you fail at it, thank God for this opportunity to show your child what it means to be teachable.

4. Spend some time journaling on the following questions: What am I afraid of? What does Jesus want

to teach me? How does he want to train me, and what grace does he desire to give me through his sacraments?

LITANY OF HUMILITY[20]

O Jesus! meek and humble of heart, hear me.
From the desire of being esteemed,
deliver me, Jesus.
From the desire of being loved ...
From the desire of being extolled ...
From the desire of being honored ...
From the desire of being praised ...
From the desire of being preferred to others ...
From the desire of being consulted ...
From the desire of being approved ...
From the fear of being humiliated ...
From the fear of being despised ...
From the fear of suffering rebukes ...
From the fear of being calumniated ...
From the fear of being forgotten ...
From the fear of being ridiculed ...
From the fear of being wronged ...
From the fear of being suspected ...
That others may be loved more than I,
Jesus, grant me the grace to desire it.
That others may be esteemed more than I ...
That, in the opinion of the world,
others may increase and I may decrease ...
That others may be chosen and I set aside ...
That others may be praised and I unnoticed ...
That others may be preferred to me in everything ...

---

20. Attributed to Rafael Cardinal Merry del Val (1865–1930), Secretary of State for Pope Saint Pius X.

That others may become holier than I, provided that I may become as holy as I should ...

SAINT-SPIRATION
Blessed Margaret of Castello

If you're still having trouble figuring out what it means to be poor in spirit, there is no greater contrast to illustrate this than that between Blessed Margaret Castello and her parents. Her wealthy parents were horrified when their child was born blind and disabled. They gave her the name Margaret but not much else, certainly no affection or comfort in her young, difficult life. In their embarrassment at Margaret's very existence, her parents told people that the child they'd expected had died at birth. They then proceeded to squirrel her away in a series of shacks, cells, and dungeons, giving her only the barest of necessities and depriving her utterly of their love. Her one consolation was that she did receive visits and the sacraments from a priest, and it was from him that she learned her true value, no matter how her parents treated her. Thus she was able to love them in spite of their incapability of returning that love.

When she reached her teens, her parents heard of a far-off town, Castello, where miracles had been reported at the tomb of a lay Franciscan. They brought her to the tomb and told her to pray there while they themselves backed away, watching, waiting for the miracle they expected God to provide. The day passed. Margaret was not visibly healed. Her parents then, without a word to Margaret, skulked silently away. They left her, their blind child, in a strange place with no earthly resources to call her own.

In time, the people of Castello softened their hearts to little Margaret. She became a lay Dominican, served the poor, and taught the rich. Abandoned by parents for not receiving the miracle they expected, Margaret herself was attended by miracles for the rest of her life, levitating while at prayer and even extinguishing a house fire with the touch of her mantle.

Where her parents were stubborn, demanding, and prideful, Margaret was gentle, generous, and teachable. Their loss. Our gain.[21]

21. Mary Perpetua, "Blessed Margaret of Castello," Catholicism.org, accessed February 16, 2021, http://catholicism.org/blessed-margaret-castello.html.

– 4 –

BLESSED ARE THEY
WHO MOURN

For They Shall Be Comforted

Beatitude Basic: Emotional Connection

*Our hope for you is firm, for we know that as you share
in the sufferings, you also share in the encouragement.*

— 2 Corinthians 1:7

When Truth Hurts

Imagine a grown man having to admit, "I've never been to a
baseball game with my dad."

This is Rick*, today a thirty-something husband and dad who
works in software development. His childhood, however, bore the
shadow of his father's mental illness. Even though both of Rick's par-

ents were overwhelmingly generous and loving, and his father admitted his illness and sought treatment, Rick still experienced legitimate loss through the effects of his father's depression and anxiety.

Regarding his dad, Rick says, "He really dislikes open public places and traveling. We've had to cancel vacations the day of because he just couldn't do it. As a small child, I just took a lot of it in stride because that was the norm, and yeah, even if we did things differently, that's just the way we were."

Rick grew up in the Midwest as an only child. In childhood, Rick's father's job necessitated a family move to the South, but this only served to isolate them further from family and friends, which exacerbated the symptoms of his father's mental illness. Rick remembers being so struck by his father's behavior that he worried he would discover that his dad had taken his own life. Thankfully, he never did, but that and other terrors weighed heavily on Rick's experience of childhood. He certainly remembers good times, like his father fixing friends' cars for them just to be kind, and as a family dropping Christmas toys off at the rectory for less fortunate children. Those warm memories, however, must exist side-by-side with his recollections of punishments for the smallest infractions, like for riding his bike around two blocks instead of one, or for receiving an A- instead of an A.

Whether through nature, nurture, or a tag team of both, Rick, too, found himself experiencing anxiety, depression, and even stomach pains similar to his father's. He remembers being a small child, having his own panic attack when his father arrived just a few minutes late to pick him up. Rather than blaming his father for any of this, however, Rick is able to see the good, even through his own pain. "With my stints of dealing with it myself, I can only say that I have a lot of respect for my dad and his struggles. And that he kept struggling. And that through it all, there are elements of an amazingly generous man that survived that crucible."

How does Rick see the pain his father's behaviors caused but still see the good too?

"My faith has carried me through it," he admits, "sometimes kicking and screaming."

Rick had faith to pull him through difficulties he had with a father who loved Rick selflessly. Yet, his father had a mental illness, which was neither Rick's nor his father's fault. This still left young, vulnerable Rick with an experience of legitimate loss. He wanted to have memories of going places with his dad, but he doesn't. He didn't get the past he wanted. He did and does, however, still experience blessing — the unique blessing that comes from God's comfort, available through the relationship Rick maintains with God through faith. Let's look at how honestly felt grief doesn't destroy our relationships with God and others but strengthens them. We cannot find true comfort unless we admit that we need comforting, and as we've already discussed in the previous chapters, we are made holy through the pursuit of truth.

Grief is truth.

On-Board the Grief Train

Did you read that last sentence above, that "Grief is truth," and hear an echo of Pontius Pilate asking Our Lord, "What is truth?" Indeed, what is grief? you may be asking. This is a totally understandable survival response in anyone who survived family abuse and dysfunction. Why? Because our emotions were continually denied us. We were not permitted to express anything that did not serve our parents' whims. Some examples directly from the Badly Spirited Parent Playbook:

- Stop crying, or I'll give you something to cry about.
- Stop being so sensitive!
- Oh, come on, I was only joking!
- Daddy and I aren't happy together anymore. Don't you want us to be happy?

- Would you quit playing the victim?

You may not have heard those exact examples, but if you think back on your childhood, you can probably identify an over-all pattern of having your emotions obliterated by people who were supposed to nurture you. Nurturing a child is teaching him or her how to be fully human. Emotions are one of the most human things we can experience, and while emotions aren't in and of themselves factual, they are the red flags and road signs that God has planted in our hearts to guide us toward the truth. Anyone who is denied an experience and understanding of her own emotions, easy and difficult, is denied her birthright. Anyone who has inconsistently or never experienced the rupture/repair cycle can't experience God's gift of relationship resurrection.

Thus, I arrived at this Beatitude, "Blessed are they who mourn, for they shall be comforted," a bit stymied. What is mourning? What is comfort? Why does Jesus promise us the second in an-swer to the first? How can I identify the features of my own emo-tional landscape when I grew up with emotional blinders placed firmly over my eyes to prevent me from "causing" anyone else the discomfort of empathy? And if our very own parents did not have any desire to offer us real comfort, who on earth would?

There are many books on grief. A deep analysis of its stag-es lies beyond the scope of this particular book. Still, one of my favorite definitions of grief, both as emotion and as process, can be found in *Grieving: Inviting God Into My Pain* by J. Catherine Sherman. Sherman states that grief is surrendering one's right to the past one had expected, and in that surrender, making space to build a new future. She further describes grief as a two-part process. The first is *retreat*: the inward-dwelling that may look like a surrender but is in fact a gathering of resources, both physical and spiritual, that enable the mourner to face future battles. The second is *journey*: that this active definition of grief moves us from where we are to where God wishes to take us next. This approach also allows grief to be what it is, when it is, and not an allowance made for people who've only experienced specific losses, like the actual, physical death of a loved one. Grief seen this way admits the truth of the pain of any loss of how things were supposed to be.[22]

Our faith tells us from the very beginning — and I'm talking the Book of Genesis beginning here — that family abuse and dysfunction are exactly not how things were supposed to be. In creating humans for each other, God's plan was not just for us to be less alone but specifically to *help* each other (Gn 2:18) within the context of a cleaving marriage that becomes the flesh of children: a family of helpers. Saint John Paul II, in his 1994 Letter to Families, demonstrated this by discussing how Jesus confirmed God's one-man, one-woman, one-family marriage plan in Matthew 19:6–8. "If the Master confirms it 'now,' he does so in order to make clear and unmistakable to all, at the dawn of the New Covenant, the indissoluble character of marriage as the basis of *the common good of the family*" (emphasis mine).[23]

So we see what the plan was, and it was a good plan, but more often we see how people fail the plan, especially when an overall failure of that plan shapes the bulk not just of our earliest memories, but bruises every emotion that we experience. Of course, part of that very experience of failure of God's plan for family complicates the experience of trying to heal from those bruises. I'm talking about the opposite of rupture/repair, which is rugsweeping: the act of pretending that something difficult didn't happen.

Dysfunctional parents deny their children's feelings. We humans are designed for rupture/repair, and so we are designed to cry until we are comforted; any tears driven underground are bound to resurface. Skilled parents face that hurt, own it when it

---

22. J. Catherine Sherman, Ph.D., *Grieving: Inviting God Into My Pain* (iUniverse, 2011), ix–x.
23. John Paul II, Letter to Families (Vatican: Libreria Editrice Vaticana, 1994), par. 7.

is caused by parental sin, and do what they can to repair any rupture because they're more invested in their children's hearts than in their own parental egos.

Dysfunctional parents don't work that way. They operate on the flawed belief that they can completely cover up any bad feelings that twinge at them. They deny, deny, deny. Thus their children learn that they will not be heard by the people who are most supposed to love them. Such children then question their emotions. Children raised this way learn to deny as well — to sweep their hurt, and sometimes others', under the rug.

Alas, there is no rug so good that it will make anything actually disappear. Rugsweeping is not comfort, not really. Jesus even points out how Moses himself tried letting the Israelites sweep relationship sins under the rug — the rug, in this case, of divorce. In Matthew 19, the Pharisees argue with Jesus about whether or not divorce is good, citing that Moses allowed men to write their own bills of divorce. Jesus, however, comes back with the reality that Moses made them that allowance, not God, and Moses only did so "because of the hardness of your hearts." As John Paul II elaborates in his Letter to Families: "'[A] man leaves his father and his mother and cleaves to his wife, and they become one flesh' (Gn 2:24). In the Gospel, Christ, disputing with the Pharisees, quotes these same words and then adds: 'So they are no longer two but one flesh. What therefore God has joined together, let not man put asunder' (Mt 19:6). In this way, he reveals anew the binding content of a fact which exists 'from the beginning' (Mt 19:8) and which always preserves this content."[24]

God's plan for the family is an indissoluble good, a community of help — a plan for attunement with repair of any ruptures that may occur. When humans fail that plan through any variety of selfishness and sin, we hurt each other. Our human inclination is to sweep that hurt under the rug, whether that rug is intim-

---

24. John Paul II, Letter to Families, 7.

idation, rage, withdrawal, or literal divorce. Jesus points out for us, in both Matthew 19 and in this particular Beatitude, that God doesn't want us to sweep under the rug all the ways people have failed us (and all the ways we've failed people, but we're getting to that). God does not rugsweep because rugsweeping is untrue, and God will do nothing that isn't of himself — nothing that isn't truth. Instead he gives us examples of how to look straight on at that pain others caused us and build a new future out of it. He wants to redeem our pain. He wants us to rise with him and not stay swept under a rug — or into a tomb. Honest grief allows us, with God's truthful help, to create a new future from a past that should not have been.

Lifting the Corner of the Rug
In this Beatitude, "Blessed are they who mourn," Jesus asks us to look at our feelings, the very feelings our dysfunctional up-bringing trained us to deny. First, Jesus asks us to love him. Then he asks us to love both neighbor and self. Next he asks us to be poor in spirit, to be teachable. How does mourning fit in as a next sensible step? Once we have been awakened to godly, self-less love and the wisdom such love teaches us, only then can our hearts become disposed to dealing honestly and virtuously with our passions, as the *Catechism* (thanks to generous input from Saint Thomas Aquinas and Saint Augustine) more clearly calls that human phenomenon of emotion (see 1762–75). Without a sense of the good of the other, and without a willingness to learn from our feelings, any grief we experience only tempts us toward destruction.

Each Beatitude has two parts: the pain and the blessing, the ashes before the beauty. Jesus tells us in this Beatitude not that we must *be* something (like poor in spirit, peacemakers) or *have something done* to us (like being persecuted for the sake of righteousness). Here he tells us we must *feel* something. I cannot help but think this is especially significant to those of us who grew up swept under the rug, burdened under our parents' misattunement, lost to the benefits of the rupture/repair cycle.

As we discussed in the last chapter, habitual sinners like abusers lack poverty of spirit. They are not willing to face the fact that they have done any wrong, especially grievous, generation-crushing wrong. Thus habitual sinners do all they can to suppress any evidence of their sin. A victim's emotions are the most pernicious evidence that he suffers from another's sin. The best way an abuser knows how to suppress this evidence is to deny any feelings these sins caused the victims. If you don't believe me, see the list I provided earlier in this chapter of characteristic things said by wrongly spirited parents to squash their children's emotional expression. Survivors of family dysfunction grow up being told not to *feel* because expression of those feelings might cause the wrongly spirited parents the discomfort of empathy. Suppressing our feelings became an integral part of our survival. We were habitually denied the blessings of this Beatitude because we were so often told we were not allowed to feel pain.

I don't want to glorify emotionality, but in this Beatitude Jesus makes it pretty clear that our feelings, especially our pain, are not a liability. They are a blessing. How do they bless us? Emotions may not tell us facts, but they are, in and of their existence, factual. When we have been hurt, emotions tell us that there may be danger ahead, who and where is safe or not. Emotions also tell us when we have something good and joyful to share with others that will help us form even richer bonds with them.

Our abusers emotionally shackled us. When we come to adulthood with our feelings still in those chains, our ability to read the meanings behind those emotions and act rightly on them becomes deeply compromised. It follows that our ability to teach our own children how to read the meaning of their own emotional lives may be painfully compromised as well. Unless we reclaim in

Christ our God-given right to our emotions, we lock ourselves in the cycle we are so desperately trying to escape. Besides, without connection to our emotions, we are cut off from the experience of joy. Emotions matter.

In order to teach our children to gain the blessing promised by Jesus, we must teach them how to read their feelings rightly. We teach them by example, which means we need to identify, accept, and express our own emotions. Then (well, usually simultaneously) we teach our own children by naming the feelings we see them express, giving them the tools not only to identify their inner emotional lives but to connect through the gift of empathy. (Check the Beatitude Basics section for some practical exercises.) As for teaching by example, we need to feel the very feelings our families of origin denied us.

We must develop practices of modeling healthy emotional expression through our own behavior. Learning to mourn may be the most cycle-breaking part of parenting because that denial of pain has been so deeply ground into our psyches. But learn it we must. Jesus asks this of us and promises us a blessing if we do. In other words, God asks us in this Beatitude to live the rupture/ repair cycle within ourselves. He asks us to become self-attuned. He asks us to be made new through the very pain we've tried so long to escape.

While it lies beyond the scope of this particular book to provide an in-depth conversation about discovering the truth of one's own emotions, there are a number of helpful resources listed in the back of this book. Individual counseling with a well-qualified, trusted therapist possessed of a well-formed conscience is also a powerful tool the survivor can use to learn how to identify and express feelings in healthy, effective ways.

Perhaps the reason our friend Rick from the beginning of this chapter was able to stay connected with his faith and his family of origin is because his father, in the end, did not deny his mental illness. He felt his feelings and got help when he needed it. For many of us, though, the story is different, especially when it comes to looking for that comfort that Jesus promises.

Even Better Than the Real Thing, Child

We humans are social animals. Earthworms don't cry out for help when they've been hurt or scared, but, unless we've had that instinct trained out of us, we children of God sure do. Comfort for our pain is one of the ways we are designed to build relationships with each other. However, in case you've forgotten, this is a fallen world. Sin has poisoned how we respond to God's designs for us. It's almost the nature of family dysfunction to destroy the rupture/repair cycle. A dark family past by default includes an experience of having one's earliest requests for comfort met with anger, mockery, silence, abandonment, or other outright cruelty. People taught us that people won't give us comfort — the comfort that we can only receive from people. This opens us up to seeking false comfort.

What do I mean by false comfort? I'm talking addictions and other forms of self-destruction. Alcohol. Drugs. Shopping. Overeating. Cutting. Trichotillomania (look that one up, if you need to). We may be tempted to think of addiction as a new phenomenon, but even Aquinas wrote about our tendency to seek false comfort when he was writing about the sin of sloth. He calls sloth a spiritual sadness, a shunning of what is good because it may not provide immediate comfort. As abuse survivors, we may have learned how to comfort ourselves, but even this learning itself can be disordered because the natural order of the family is for parents to comfort their children, certainly not the reverse. Aquinas wasn't the first to write about disordered comfort either. He goes back to Aristotle, "The Philosopher," and points out the reality that, "Those who find no joy in spiritual pleasures[,] have recourse to the pleasures of the body."[25]

---

25. Aquinas, *ST,* II-II, q.35, a.4.

There is much joy that comes from having a troubled spirit receive genuine comfort from people who want to bring the love of Christ to us. Many of us reach adulthood without having a sensate experience of that joy. I am one of those people. I was slogging through the writing of this chapter, utterly stymied by the idea of having to write about comfort for mourning when, honestly, I haven't experienced much of it myself. The most reliable form of comfort I'd found in life was food. Through the years, I've often thanked the Lord for letting food be my addiction because, by all rights, someone who's experienced the childhood I have should be dead in a gutter with a needle in her arm. By God's mercy, I'm a binge eater instead.

That said, while tackling this chapter, I found myself asking my therapist, who also works in drug and alcohol rehab, if he happened to have any insight into how I could tackle my food addiction. I told him I'm not overweight because I don't know how to eat nutritiously; that's why countless diets didn't work for me. I'm overweight because I don't know how to stop eating — because I'm an addict.

"You need accountability," was his reply.

I don't know about you, but I hear the word "accountability" and I think of a pair of guys in a Bible study who get together for coffee once a week and are "accountable" to each other. For what? I have no idea. So I asked.

"What does accountability even look like?"

"Well," he said, "with my other clients, I have them identify their triggers — like, they're going to drive into an area of town where they usually use. They call their sponsor before they go there, then they call again after they get through it."

I left that appointment with homework: list the events and feelings that trigger my binges, then look for an accountability source. A few days later, I found an app for addicts of all kinds, even people with eating disorders. This app includes a way to send out a call for help when you feel like "using" your substance. Then, day or night, someone else on the app is there to help you say no to false comfort. What did I have to lose?

The first time I used the app to reach out, I was alone and uncomfortable and wanted to binge so badly, but I also was so tired of failing. I reached out using the app's anonymous "lifeline," and a few minutes later I was texting with another addict. He (possibly she?) responded with simple encouragement and ideas for facing the craving that I was too anxious to be able to think of myself. He didn't say anything earth-shattering: take deep breaths, drink water, that sort of thing. Neither did he berate me for being stupid enough to let food run my life. He was simply there at no benefit to himself when I needed to know I wasn't alone.

Best of all, he believed in me. In a way, he provided the fathering I had never received from my own father. He provided the love of God the Father to me in a way I would not have found had I not fallen into an addiction. I'm not saying that my years of seeking false comfort through food were years well-spent. No, they are years lost to gluttony and all the bad fruit that sin produces: shame, poor health, poor example to my children, and dishonesty in my relationships. Still, moment by moment, our God delivers beauty through ashes. He promises us that, when we actually mourn our pain instead of hiding from it, he will send us comfort.

So that's what I did that day when I reached out through the app's lifeline. And I've done so repeatedly since then. That was in 2019, when I first began my recovery from food addiction. As of this writing, I have gained food sobriety, lost more than 80 percent of what I need to lose to get to a healthy weight, and I've gained an army of recovery buddies who never fail to be God's comfort for me — and, hopefully, I for them. That isn't all I've lost and gained, however. I've also gained the experience of being able to tolerate my own discomforts, accepting truth instead of reaching for food. This has helped me be more present for my children in their own big emotions, when they need comfort. I've been able to experience self-attunement, which has freed me to be more present and attuned to my own children's needs and experiences. Success of this type has multiplied my experience of joy in my relationships with those closest to me, in my relationship with myself, and most obviously in my relationship with God.

Here is where I must admit, however, that providing my own children comfort is still an area in which I have a lot of room for growth. Of course, children need to receive comfort in ways that are respectful of their developmental ages, temperaments, and any number of factors, but what really seems to foster emotional connection between parent and child (even the parent I am and the children I have) no matter the age is the gift of validation. The antithesis of rugsweeping, validation is just the acknowledgment of a child's emotion, acceptance of that child's right to have that emotion right now, and a parent's refusal to do anything to make that child's emotional experience go away, no matter how big or unmanageable it might seem in the moment. If you'd like to learn more about the importance and practice of validation for attunement and emotional connection, please consider the books listed in the Resources section.

As humans made in the image and likeness of God, comfort for our sorrow is our birthright, but our fallen families of origin failed us. That is their sin. That is their loss. In Mark 10:30, however, he promises us that when we give up everything and follow him, we may be persecuted, but we will receive "a hundred times more now in this present age: houses and brothers and sisters and mothers and children and lands." That "more" will come to us when he knows we need it most.

For me, it came to help me write this chapter. It came in time to give me a hope I'm now privileged to share with you — the hope of being made completely new.

Will It Always Hurt?

As I was writing in circles, asking God how to finish this chapter on mourning and comfort, I received a new issue of *eLumen*, the electronic newsletter for my province of Dominican laity.[26] It was our first issue for the Easter season, and there was an article on the Third Part of the *Summa Theologiae*, "On the Treatise of the Incarnation, Article 4: Whether Christ's body ought to have risen with its scars?" After all, Aquinas reasons through Scripture and Church Fathers, aren't scars signs of corruption and disintegration? Once the cause of something painful stops, shouldn't its effects disappear as well, for redemption to be fulfilled? Shouldn't Jesus be able to get rid of his own woundedness? And if he can't, does that mean we are eternally doomed to our wounds as well?

Aquinas banishes this fear by citing Saint Bede, Saint Augustine, and yet more Scripture to tell us that Jesus could do no less than rise glorified with his scars. His wounds prove to us his identity, his mercy, his compassion. "The scars that remained in Christ's body belong neither to corruption nor defect, but to the greater increase of glory, inasmuch as they are the trophies of His power; and a special comeliness will appear in the places scarred by the wounds."[27]

When we model ourselves after Christ by seeking to love others through our suffering, we will still bear wounds. Those wounds, however, will be transformed into evidence of how God brought us through agony into everlasting love. Will we always hurt the way we hurt at our parents' hands? Oh, my friends, if you want to read the fulfillment of God's promise to comfort the

---

26. Saint Joseph Province, Eastern USA, "eLumen," LayDominicans.org, accessed February 16, 2021, https://laydominicans.org/about-us/elumen/.

27. Aquinas, *Summa, ST*, III, q.54, a.4.

mourning, go read Revelation 21. That's the chapter in which John sees the old earth pass and the new arrive, where God will be with us to be the father we were supposed to have from the beginning, the one who wipes our tears and brings us life and joy. Revelation promises us that we may yet cry, but we will be restored to the rupture/repair cycle through that pain. God himself will dry our tears with perfect love. This chapter, however, reminds us to dedicate ourselves to the truth now, even the sometimes-painful truth of our own feelings and our children's, because "deceivers of every sort" will end in "the burning pool of fire and sulfur, which is the second death."

Mourning is truth, the opposite of deceit. That grief may scorch now, but when we refuse to deceive anyone, including ourselves, about the depths of anyone's grief, including our children's, our parents', and our own, we free ourselves to let God repair us. Truthful mourning only leads to comfort. Jesus promised.

A Whole New Land

As we discussed in the last chapter, the root of child abuse is not a family dynamic or even a cultural one. If that were the root, you would have no hope, for you would be doomed to continuing the cycle that birthed your pain. No, the root of child abuse is personal sin. God, the just judge and perfect father, by his very nature, could never bear to erase the evidence of others' sins against us. He will never deny us our feelings because they reveal truth. If we want to receive the comfort denied us by our fallen parents, we must pursue truth, teach our children to pursue truth, and pursue personal holiness at all costs. I venture to say that this is why our friend Rick at the beginning of this chapter, despite his father's mental illness and his own, has been able to hold on to his faith and be comforted by it. His father never denied causing Rick pain, so that pain was not so compounded by sin as it is in the victims of habitual abusers. Our abhorrence of sin will only benefit our children's spiritual and mental well-being.

However, our culture frequently warns us against "pushing our religion" on our children, doesn't it? Isn't forcing our beliefs on our children somehow disrespectful of their autonomy? Maybe some of you reading this had parents who misused Scripture and faith traditions to control you, obliterate your feelings, and deny you your humanity — and so the thought of encouraging your children to pursue holiness is discomfiting. Or maybe you're simply scarred from your experience of being controlled by your parents that any exhortation to teach your children holiness makes you shake in your parenting boots.

Whatever trepidation you're feeling at this point, feel it, and don't shy away from it. God is letting you experience that trepidation for a reason. It's his way of alerting you that he wants to change things for you, so that you can live more fully and freely in him, more joyfully with your family of origin and your children, no matter how they treat you in the moment. That said, if God is preparing us to live this joy while simultaneously feeling whatever feelings we might experience, comfortable or otherwise, it's only natural to wonder just as Mary did at the Annunciation, "How can this be?" How can we be people who feel both pain and joy? How can we become like Mary, who at the cross was both Our Lady of Sorrows and Our Lady of Hope?

This is possible through the next Beatitude, which promises an inheritance for the meek. By teaching us what meekness is and isn't, God makes a way for us to live the truth of both joy and sorrow, so that we are no longer constrained by human expectation but are free to make the most of what we do have. Meekness — and the boundaries gifted with that beatitude — opens up to us a whole new land.

HOLY FAMILY MOMENT
Jesus' Triumphal Entry into Jerusalem (Lk 19:28–40)

At last, Jesus is receiving the recognition he deserves. He's arriving in Jerusalem to a roaring crowd who are falling over themselves to make his entry as comfortable and glorious as possible. Joseph has passed on by this point, so he's not there to see it, but Mary is. She sees her son being glorified by the people he loves as best they can. Even now, though, the Pharisees want to sweep joy under the rug. They tell Jesus, "Rebuke your disciples!" Jesus answers, "I tell you, if they keep silent, the stones will cry out."

In pain and joy, truth cannot be silenced. Luke's account of the first Palm Sunday mentioned the nearness of the Mount of Olives. Jesus is God. Jesus knows the future. Jesus knows he's about to get much different than what he deserves. He will mourn that injustice on the Mount he's passing now, to the cheers of his people.

Jesus and Mary know exactly how it feels to hurt because the people who were supposed to love you and your child do the exact opposite. Our Savior and his mother put their pain to work, on and by the cross, respectively. That pain bore something new and eternally healing for all of us.

BEATITUDE BASIC WORKSHOP
Emotional Connection

1. In your journal, begin a practice of writing every morning about one thing that happened to you in the previous day, and identify any of the emotions you experienced as a result. How did your body express that emotion: clenched fists, yelling, laughing, sighing, eye-rolling? Don't judge whether you should have had that emotion or not. Just let the truth of that experience exist in your memory. Bring each of these journal entries to Jesus, and ask him if there is someone in

       your life with whom you could share them, such as a
       spouse or trusted friend.

2.   Fill your family's emotional connection toolbox: Practice naming emotions with your children. This can be done in silly ways (getting a book of emoji stickers and naming the emotion shown by each face) or in the moment, by saying things like, "You sound angry because your toy broke," or "I feel disappointed today because my plant died, and I tried so hard to keep it alive." Provide yourself and your family with healthy comfort rather than any kind of rugsweeping. If emotional connection is new to you, developing this skill will take time. It will always take practice.

3.   Examine your life for signs you are seeking false comfort, then with God's help, take action to combat that tendency. Talk with a trusted friend, spiritual advisor, and/or qualified therapist about how addiction may be affecting your life and your family. See the Resources section of this book for suggestions.

4.   Connect with or form a support group that helps you work your way through your emotional landscape and provides the genuine comfort God wants to send you even in this life.

PRAYER TO SAINT MICHAEL THE ARCHANGEL

Saint Michael the Archangel, defend us in battle, be our protection against the wickedness and snares of the devil. May God rebuke him, we humbly pray; and do thou, O Prince of the Heavenly host, by the power of God, cast into hell Satan and all the evil spirits who prowl about the world seeking the ruin of souls. Amen.

SAINT-SPIRATION

Saint Zélie Martin

If there were to be a patron saint of cycle-breakers, it might be Saint Zélie Martin. Zélie would become the mother of Saint Thérèse of Lisieux, the Church's beloved "Little Flower," but Zélie herself had a childhood empty of comfort. Her father was a grouch, and her mother was cold, refusing even to allow Zélie to own a doll of her own. Zélie's childhood was plagued with headaches on top of her parents' distance and criticism. In her own words, Zélie's childhood was "as sad as a shroud." *Et encore*, and yet, Saint Zélie Martin was an apple who fell blessedly far from her tree. She developed a pious reliance on God's providence. She grew up to endure countless parenting hardships, such as the loss of four children, and the discovery that one daughter was being abused by a family servant. Through all of this and her own eventual suffering and death from breast cancer, she made herself a model of affection, stability, and faith for her children.[28]

---

28. Helene Mongin, *The Extraordinary Parents of Saint Therese of Lisieux*, translated by Marsha Daigle-Williamson (Huntington, IN: Our Sunday Visitor, 2015), 15–23.

— 5 —

BLESSED ARE THE MEEK

For They Will Inherit the Land

Beatitude Basic: Boundaries
With all vigilance guard your heart,
for in it are the sources of life.
— Proverbs 4:23

Pity Party

I cringe at the very thought of what I'm about to write, but there's such an important parenting lesson about meekness in this memory that I owe it to you to share it. This is the story of my tenth birthday party. I wanted to have a sleepover party. I wasn't the most popular person in my grade, to say the least, so I only wanted to invite the two girls I could call friends. My father, however, got two ideas in his head. First, if I were to have a sleepover party, I had to invite every single girl in my grade — even the ones who regularly bullied or excluded me. Second, my father didn't want it to look like I was grubbing for presents, so I wasn't allowed to tell people it was a birthday party. No cake, no presents, just … just what? I don't even remember. My father's stipulations made me extremely uncomfortable, but my comfort meant nothing to my father, and he had long since created a world where no one was permitted to tell him he might be wrong without facing his rage. Thus I had my not-a-birthday-party sleepover.

In a validation of my not-so-popular status, less than half of the girls in my grade came; neither of my two best friends made it. There was an awkward moment where two of the attendees had known it was my birthday and brought presents in spite of being told not to do so. This wasn't the worst part of the experience, though. Our family had not yet acquired that newfangled invention the VCR, so there was no movie to watch to keep people distracted from tween girl drama. Thus, after the pizza and cheese curls had been eaten, all the other girls separated into their exclusive groups. I, the hostess (I can't say "guest of honor" because, you know, it wasn't a birthday party), was left alone and lonely in her own home. I don't know how it came to her attention, but my mother caught me crying in a corner at my own not-birthday-party.

The week before this event, my same-age cousin and myself, inspired by the leadup to the 1984 Summer Olympics, had made rhythmic gymnastics "ribbons" for ourselves out of crepe streamers and old Lincoln Logs roof shingles. Then we developed our own rhythmic gymnastics routine (to Michael Jackson's "PYT: Pretty Young Thing," if you're looking for another timestamp). We'd performed this for our families, and I'd even been practicing it just for fun (and maybe for the daydream of having an Olympic sport at which I might not be guaranteed utter failure).

"Do your ribbon routine," my mother insisted. "That will get their attention."

I obeyed. I put my vinyl *Thriller* album on the turntable, found the groove for "PYT," and did my half of that ribbon routine.

The voices in the room fell silent at first. It wasn't terribly long before I could see the sideways smirks my guest peers were giving each other. However, my mom had told me to do this, and she was another person who punished any disagreement. I finished the routine to some very pathetic applause, then went back into the kitchen to find more food. The story of my performance made it back to school on Monday, and the smirks turned to outright laughter and mocking. The boys of our grade gleefully joined in. My misery grew. Mom was right: It certainly got their attention.

I couldn't understand what went wrong. Weren't people supposed to applaud performances and fawn over the performer, not ridicule her? Didn't I do everything my parents had told me to? If I was being a good girl and doing everything I was supposed to do, why was I so humiliated, lonely, and hated? Now, many years free of my parents' flawed influence, I see exactly what went wrong. That stunt showed my guests, young as we all may have been, that I didn't care about them as people but rather wanted attention for myself. In all aspects of that party debacle, my parents demonstrated that they had never learned what it meant to be meek, how to value meekness as a necessary part of genuine, connected relationships. Thus they were never able to teach me how to live my way into the blessings promised by this Beatitude.

You may have found that last paragraph contradictory. Wasn't I being unquestioningly obedient? Isn't unquestioning obedience the very definition of meekness? It's not. Let me show you why.

A Bad Routine

Let's quickly check back on the Beatitude Basics we've discovered in the previous chapters. With love of God, we received confidence in our worth. With love of neighbor and self, we received compassion. Teachability came with poverty of spirit, and mourning gave us a connection to our emotional lives. Meekness, when properly lived, takes all of those staples and uses them to establish boundaries between ourselves and others, so that we obey when necessary without being tyrannized, we can let go of those things that aren't our responsibility, and when that letting go leaves us lonely (which sometimes it will), we are confident enough in our own worth as God's beloved creations that the loneliness can't break us. We can say yes and no with confidence that we will be safe and honored by all to whom our worth is precious. We also will be able to guard our hearts (see the verse that opened this chapter) from those who are afraid to care for the life the heart gives. We will have self-control, and we will lose the desire to control others. God's love tells us that we need boundaries. Meekness creates and maintains them.

You probably find this a weird way of looking at meekness. Isn't meekness saying "yes" when everything in you is screaming "no"? Yes and no, especially for survivors of family abuse. At the party described above, there were several failures of meekness, but all of them looked at first blush like people being "nice," "considerate," "good," and "obedient." Really, they were signs of poor boundaries. I mean, wasn't it "nice" to invite every single girl in my grade to the party? Actually, it wasn't, because the invitation was made in an effort to exert control over how people perceived our family. Wasn't it "considerate" to tell people it wasn't a birthday party and not to bring presents? Alas, that instruction was just another attempt to control other people's choices. Wasn't it "good" to want a lonely, hurting child to feel less pain? Plainly, no: The solution offered, to put on a show, only taught the lonely, hurting child to demand attention, not to make genuine connections with the people around her by finding out more about them and showing *them* welcome and care.

This is why growth in meekness fills our parenting pantries with healthy boundaries. As we discussed when looking at God's command to love your neighbor as yourself, we see that love honors where one individual ends and the other begins. This love is expressed through meekness because meekness is that function of holiness that keeps us from trying to use our emotions to control others, and it helps us to deny others any perceived right to control us with their emotions. Meekness teaches us to empathize with others' pain while still honoring our own. Meekness empowers us to empathize with another's pain without owning it. Meekness makes room for joy in all relationships, even when one person is for whatever reason not giving the other what he needs.

Abuse of meekness powers the cycle that is generational abuse. A bad parent refuses to own her own pain because that pain scares her. Rather, she passes the pain onto her child and expects that young, dependent soul to provide the remedy for that pain. This parent has power that this child does not have at this stage of life and uses that power to control the child rather than to love. This is unnatural (see Col 3:21; CCC 2206) and usually results in the child's resentment. That child grows up to become a parent, and now the new grandchild/child has pains the new child/parent actually has a responsibility to remedy, like hunger, loneliness, and bandages for cuts. This is the natural order. However, the new parent is still resentful over the false burden he carries on behalf of his parent. He thinks he is powerless because he was trained to see himself so in order to continue satisfying the unfair demands of his then-more-powerful parent. Now here's this helpless child, making the same demands for comfort that the out-of-control parent made on this new parent when he was a child. The new parent actually has more power than the child and knows no better than to use that power to control rather than love the child. Instead of soothing a crying child, the new parent is in grave danger of replaying the old tapes: *Stop being such a baby. Can't you see I'm busy? I'll give you something to cry about.*

Shame, blame, rage. Lather, rinse, repeat. The cycle begins again, unless that cycle is broken. The old ways stay old unless we turn them over to the God who can make them new.

Real Estate

There's something distinctly powerful for abuse survivors in this Beatitude. Jesus promises those who live meekness an inheritance: the land. What does "land" mean, anyway? Well, the first thing that comes to mind is the Promised Land, the land God pledged to the descendants of Abraham and the Israelite slaves who fled Egypt. To the people of Jesus' time, inheriting land meant freedom from Roman tyranny. To people of all ages, faiths, and cultures, ownership of land means power, the opportunity to acquire wealth and stability for those who are willing to put in the work. If you own your land and don't pay rent or a mortgage on it, you have a freedom that renters don't have. Land means safety. Land means a home of one's own. To the one "inheriting the land," an inheritance is something freely given, not earned, something received by right of kinship.

In many ways, "land" represents self-control. What Jesus called land, then, seems to be what psychologists call *locus of control*.

Locus of control is a concept first identified by American psychologist Julian Rotter. Locus of control refers to how a person identifies the wellspring of what happened to him in the past, what is happening to him now, and what might happen to him in the future. Let's say a person has survived a tornado but his house and business did not. Can this survivor accurately identify what was not within his control (where the tornado landed) and what remains in his control (how he chooses to rebuild)? Through years of research, Rotter and his colleagues discovered that people tend to view adversity primarily either as something against which they are overwhelmingly helpless or as something they can navigate successfully through their choices. One's locus of control falls at some point along a continuum from *internal* to *external*. When one has a mostly *internal* locus of control, one tends to see most things that occur to them as being manageable through their own personal choices. With a mostly *external* locus of control, a person tends to see his life experience as being mostly out of his control. A person whose locus of control leans external blames others and shuns responsibility; a person whose locus of control leans internal finds and takes opportunities to improve his situation through personal responsibility. Researchers further discovered that people operating mostly from an internal locus of control were better able to thrive after hardships ranging from job difficulties to war to, well, tornadoes. Today, an internal locus of control might more commonly be referred to as a "growth mindset."[29]

None of this should be shocking, since we know God's word. Jesus promises us that if we remain in his word, we will know truth, and through truth, be made free (see Jn 8:31–32). Truth sets us free because it convinces us that we cannot change things outside of our power, but we can change those things under our purview. Seeing the world with a healthy internal locus of control is seeing with the eyes of truth: identifying what we can change, what we can't, and knowing the difference, as the old Serenity Prayer goes. The converse, of course, is also true: When we insist that we have no control over our choices, not only are we lying to ourselves and others, but we trap ourselves into a poisonous loop of self-defeat in order to continue convincing ourselves of the lie that we are utterly helpless in the face of our circumstances. The external locus of control says, "I'd hurt less if people would stop complaining about how I've hurt them." The parent operating from an external locus of control lives in terror of having to face reality.

Former music journalist turned Catholic author Dawn Eden has seen this terror at work in her own mother. Before coming to

---

29. Herbert M. Lefcourt, "Locus of Control" in *Encyclopedia of Psychology*, ed. Alan E. Kazin (Washington, DC: American Psychological Association and Oxford University Press, 2000), 5:68–70.

faith in Christ, Eden lived hard, overwhelming her own sensory experiences in order to escape a childhood full of memories of being used by the adults who should have loved her. She now covers topics like the pain and triumph experienced by faith-filled survivors of abuse and dysfunction. Eden writes about how her mother's lack of meekness not only led to her inability to provide young Dawn with safety, but also how her mother's failure to embrace healthy boundaries even now prevents her from seeing Dawn's pain. As we discussed in the last chapter, blindness to another's pain is blindness to another's soul and leads to shallow, unfulfilling relationships. This is especially painful when the ideal of the relationship is a close and nurturing one, such as parent and child.

In *My Peace I Give You*, Eden takes a look at her experience with her mother in light of 2 Corinthians 12:9, where Paul talks about how Jesus told him, "'My grace is sufficient for you, for power is made perfect in weakness.' I will rather boast most gladly of my weaknesses, in order that the power of Christ may dwell with me." Eden keeps this verse in mind when she encounters her own mother's inability to "remember" any part she played in the sexual abuse Eden suffered as a child. She writes, "The people who are truly weakest are often those who put forth a false front of impenetrability. They live in fear that their imperfections will be discovered, like gods of iron with feet of clay. I see this now in my mother, who has worked desperately to keep up the image of being a 'perfect mom.'" Eden then describes some ways her mother failed to provide healthy nurturing. "Even now, I feel, her resistance to my memories of abuse — the worst of which I remember being perpetrated in front of her by one of her boyfriends — is fueled by her fear of vulnerability."[30]

A parent with an external locus of control would blame Eden's abuse on others and accept no responsibility for putting one's own

---

30. Dawn Eden, *My Peace I Give You: Healing Sexual Wounds with the Help of the Saints* (Notre Dame, IN: Ave Maria Press, 2012), xxviii.

daughter knowingly in harm's way. Some parents, however, take that helpless view one step further and deny that anything bad even happened, denying the sin so deeply that they themselves have "forgotten" their failings. This is why an internal locus of control, even in the face of our own grave failings, shows how "power is made perfect in weakness." Parents in denial think they are appearing more powerful, when in fact, if they would just admit their sins against their own children, they would have the power that comes from not having to hide anything. They would inherit the land.

God knows Eden's frustration and ours. He asks, "Did you eat from the forbidden tree?" We answer, "She gave it to me, so I ate it!" and "The serpent tricked me!" Clearly, Adam and Eve at that moment of having their sin discovered demonstrated external locus of control. An internal locus of control, however, doesn't just help us avoid sin ("You know, I can choose to obey God and not eat the fruit he told me not to"), but also helps to experience and express remorse for when we do sin. Remorse also is truth, and probably a harder truth to face than one's own victimhood at the hands of others. Remorse, however, just might be the most healing side of truth. Remorse heals broken relationships, as we see in the story of the Prodigal Son, when the returning child tells his father, "I have sinned against heaven and against you; I no longer deserve to be called your son" (Lk 15:21). The father responds by welcoming him back, not as a slave, but as a son. Remorse further forges space for new relationships to grow. We see this when Simon Peter tells Jesus, "Depart from me, Lord, for I am a sinful man." How does Jesus respond? He tells Peter not to fear but to follow him into a new future (see Lk 5:8–10).

And that's why I had to bring up locus of control in a chapter on meekness. How often were you, as a child, blamed for things that weren't your fault? You misbehaved, so Dad had to hit you. You stressed Mom out; no wonder she drinks. A sexually abusive parent may have convinced his or her victim child that the child brought the abuse on him or herself for being "dirty." In the event your abusive parent or parents ever faced real consequences for their actions, especially if you're the one who told, you may have been blamed for "ruining the family." Growing up steeped in such lies can twist how we perceive reality. We might become pushovers, telling ourselves and our children that we can't control anything, not even ourselves. We may have learned the blame and shame game from our families of origin, passing down to yet another generation the falsehood that the children are responsible for the parents. That is not God's playbook for the Fourth Commandment. Truth is. Freedom is. Love is.

Imagine a parent who has made a parenting mistake: say, punishing a child too harshly. A parent with a healthy internal locus of control will recognize that he is the parent, the child is not, and will apologize to God for this sin, apologize directly to the child for this sin without expressing any blame toward the child, and then seek to make amends and restore the parent-child relationship to a place of trust. This is the parent practicing meekness, adding life and depth to the rupture/repair cycle. A parent with an external locus of control will excuse himself from the sin by claiming outside stress (a difficult day at work, say, or "hanger") and then will blame the child for being out of control. In the first scenario, the child learns that the parent is invested in keeping their relationship honest and free. In the second, the child learns that sins can be passed on to another person and that parents can do what they want without repercussions. This is hardly truth. This is the parent who is practicing not meekness but selfishness.

Imagine the depth of connection Dawn Eden's mother could have gained by choosing to initiate the rupture/repair cycle, compassionately admitting her failings to her daughter, owning them, and working to make what amends she could. Imagine the healing and joy she has chosen to deny herself and her daughter by choosing ongoing misattunement over true connection. Alas, she declined ownership and chose instead to remain a renter. Appearing strong, especially to ourselves, is not strength. Appearing weak in order to claim the truth, however painful that truth may be, unites us to the infinite power of Christ who is Truth.

As parents, no matter how we ourselves were parented, if we don't choose meekness, we choose weakness.

Free and Clear

We survivors of family abuse and dysfunction felt powerless as children. We felt anything but free. Today we often feel powerless against our own impulses as we parent children learning to deal with impulses of their own — impulses that incidentally can feel to our traumatized memories like the irrational demands of raging parents. And here comes Jesus and his evangelists telling us that weakness is strength and that meekness gives us safety. I know I've felt at times like the Bible was telling me I had to choose between being a doormat or a tyrant: make a choice between earthly misery or eternal misery. Yet we are made perfect in weakness because the truth is that we are imperfect. The more comfortable we get with the reality of our shortcomings, the less we have to cover them up. The less we have to fear from them. The less we fear the discomfort we get from admitting our failings, the more graceful we become about discomfort in general. The less we hide from necessary discomfort, the less likely we are to choose lies over truth, the closer we get to being like Jesus. God's power flows to others through us, made perfect in and because of our weakness.

While the words "internal locus of control" might be relatively new, they are no surprise to Jesus. In his wisdom, he knew that the best way to put hurting people back on their feet was to remind them what is theirs to control and what is not. One of the clearest instructions Christ gives us in the Gospel about how meekness works over weakness can be found in that oft-misinterpreted, oft-abused opening to Matthew 7:

Stop judging, that you may not be judged. For as you
judge, so will you be judged, and the measure with
which you measure will be measured out to you. Why
do you notice the splinter in your brother's eye, but do
not perceive the wooden beam in your own eye? How
can you say to your brother, "Let me remove that splinter from your eye," while the wooden beam is in your
eye? You hypocrite, remove the wooden beam from your
eye first; then you will see clearly to remove the splinter
from your brother's eye. (Matthew 7:1–5)

Unfortunately, this verse, designed to teach us the right way to approach sin in our lives, is used far too often for the very rugsweeping
it decries. Abusers confronted with their abuse may call upon this
verse to shut up their accusers, saying, "How dare you tell me I'm
wrong, when you're obviously not perfect either!" If we look more
closely at these verses and those that follow, we can see through any
misuse of Christ's words and clear our way to following his wisdom
into truth and freedom. In these verses, Jesus never tells us *not* to
address the sins of others, but he does tell us to address our own
sins *first*. Why, when we may have been hurt by others far more
than we ourselves have hurt them? Because Jesus wants us to have
the gift of the Holy Spirit called self-control. He wants us to have
boundaries. In the creation story, we see that we are made for each
other and from each other, but we are still separate beings with our
own choices, feelings, and responsibilities. Sin occurs when we try
to take on what is not ours to take, from the forbidden fruit to the
thoughts and feelings of others: in other words, things not given
into our control.

The Matthew verses referenced above clearly remind us of those
things within our internal locus of control. God puts self-reflection
first not to obliterate our pain but to help us identify it accurately
and prevent us from causing others pain. Jesus wants us to own our

sins and bring them to him not because he wants us to feel bad, but because he recognizes the desire of the heart that truly wants to end the generational cycle of abuse, because perhaps the worst part of abuse is the denial of the abuser. When we follow Christ's directive to first remove the plank from our own eyes, we put an end to the rugsweeping. We teach our children that they are allowed their pain when we sin against them, and we show them what the truth looks like and how to live it themselves. We teach them and ourselves not to turn into our denial-shackled abusive parents. We set our children and ourselves free, the freedom only truth can accomplish, the power that only comes when we profess our own weakness.

So how do we keep our own vision clear from our own sins? A prayer life steeped in Scripture. Supportive, honest friends. Frequent reception of the sacraments, especially confession, at least once a month, if not more. It doesn't matter if our sins are smaller than the ones our parents committed against us. Their sins are not within our control. Ours, however, are. When we feel ourselves "becoming our parents" and balking at the pain we have caused others, we owe it to ourselves and our children to return to what the psalmist calls "true sincerity." "My sin is always before me ... Behold, I was born in guilt ... Behold, you desire true sincerity; and secretly you teach me wisdom. Cleanse me ... Restore to me the gladness of your salvation" (Ps 51:5, 7–9, 14).

Mourning the hurt caused by your own sins doesn't erase the harm done to you by others. Instead this allows you to identify what guilt is yours and what is not, to release yourself from false guilt foisted on you by people who refused to mourn their own sins. This puts boundaries on your pain so that you can maintain godly meekness in spite of others' sins. Having been the victim doesn't justify our victimizing others. There's that anonymous phrase floating around that says, "If you don't heal what hurt you, you'll bleed on people who didn't cut you." This is exactly why Jesus first tells us to become poor in spirit — teachable — before we mourn. We cannot see clearly what to mourn until we are ready to learn true right from true wrong, especially when our families of origin failed to teach us these vital truths. We can be taught, however, and we can be comforted — and in that comfort, comfort our own children, teaching them that their feelings have as much value as ours should have had to our parents and that they have always had to God the Father who loves us.

But how does a father who loves us respond when others legitimately sin against us, sinners that we are? For the answer to that, let's read a little further along in Matthew 7, where we learn we are not just expected to talk about the splinters in others' eyes, but also how to determine who is feeding us good and who is not. In other words, we are going to examine the joy available to us through our hunger and thirst for what is right.

HOLY FAMILY MOMENT
The Flight into Egypt (Mt 2:13–15)

I bet Joseph was pretty furious that that earthly ruler Herod dared to come after the Son of God, given to earth in the form of a helpless human child. He could have let his anger, his idea of how things were supposed to be, flare up within him. He could have stayed and fought when the soldiers came to murder the baby who'd been entrusted to him. He would've been justified. Instead he was the guy who was quiet enough to hear God's voice in a dream of angels, and thus he got his family away to safety. That's the gift of meekness: knowing when our own way is not necessarily the best way, which, in listening silence, frees us to hear the still, small voice telling us the next right thing to do.

BEATITUDE BASIC WORKSHOP
Boundaries

1. Use your journal and take a moment to reorient yourself into an internal locus of control. Look back at the two-lists journal exercise mentioned at the end of Chapter Two. Then pick one thing from your list of things you control and write three to five ways to improve one of those things immediately. Likewise, examine the list of things out of your control and write to God about ways you can surrender those things into his care.

2. Journal about ways to establish and maintain healthy boundaries with both your parents and your children. What things can you control: the time you spend with your parents, how much internet time your teens get, suggestions for places to meet your parents, nutritious meals for your children that help them feel well-regulated? Pick one of them to put into practice. Reevaluate as needed.

3. Practice modeling healthy, blame-free apologies with your children. Show them that you frequent the Sacrament of Reconciliation. If you have trouble accepting blame when appropriate or are too eager to take blame that is not rightly yours, seek counsel from a trusted source.

THE MAGNIFICAT
(Lk 1:46–55)

My soul proclaims the greatness of the Lord;
    my spirit rejoices in God my savior.
For he has looked upon his handmaid's lowliness;
    behold, from now on will all ages call me blessed.

The Mighty One has done great things for me,
    and holy is his name.
His mercy is from age to age
    to those who fear him.
He has shown might with his arm,
    dispersed the arrogant of mind and heart.
He has thrown down the rulers from their thrones
    but lifted up the lowly.
The hungry he has filled with good things;
    the rich he has sent away empty.
He has helped Israel his servant,
    remembering his mercy,
according to his promise to our fathers,
    to Abraham and to his descendants forever.

SAINT-SPIRATION
Blessed Pier Giorgio Frassati

If you know anything about Blessed Pier Giorgio Frassati, you might wonder why he's in the chapter on meekness. He was the devout Catholic son of a wealthy, agnostic journalist, publisher and politician; Pier Giorgio also was a known prankster, a goofball who wasn't especially good at school, who was as likely to be found scaling the side of a mountain as walking into Mass. In his relationship with his family, however, it was his meekness that won the day for Christ, but this was no overnight task. In fact, it would cost Pier Giorgio his life.

Before he died at age 24, both marriage and the priesthood had been offered to him, but in deference to his family, he declined both. Sure, when morality was on the line, he stood his ground, such as giving his shoes to a beggar at the door in order to protect the beggar from Giorgio's father's wrath. However, he didn't think his parents would approve of his becoming a priest or, later, of his marrying his sweetheart who'd come from a family far too poor to run in the same social circles as the Frassatis. He deferred to his parents in this matter in spite of the fact that their own marriage was very clearly falling apart. With such turbulence at home, he did what he could to support family unity, denying his own desires but never denying the needs of the poor people he saw. Eventually, Pier Giorgio contracted polio from the poor people he'd been serving. At his funeral, his parents at last saw the outpouring of love for their son from all the people he'd helped. They were so moved by the love his life had shown that they reconciled.

Meekness heals even those who at first can't understand it.[31]

---

31. Olivia Spears, "Bl. Pier Giorgio Frassati," Catholic Exchange, December 4, 2014, https://catholicexchange.com/11-reasons-love-bl-pier-giorgio-frassati.

– 6 –

BLESSED ARE THEY WHO HUNGER AND THIRST FOR RIGHTEOUSNESS

For They Will Be Satisfied

Beatitude Basic: Sensitivity of Conscience

Vengeance is mine and recompense,
for the time they lose their footing;
Because the day of their disaster is at hand
and their doom is rushing upon them!

— Deuteronomy 32:35

How Well Do You Know God?

My friend Marissa* is a devoted cradle Catholic. She spent time in a religious order before discerning God's call to marriage and motherhood. One day I couldn't help noticing that she looked remarkably sad. I asked if she wanted to talk. She had the courage to tell me about how she had been fighting a crisis of faith ever since the Pennsylvania (our home state) grand jury report on child abuse committed by Catholic priests had been issued the previous summer.

Now my friend was telling me about how she could barely bring herself to go to Mass and adoration, doing so only for the sake of her children. When she did go, she was shocked to find herself consumed with rage. She was deeply troubled to be experiencing this level of anger in places where she had always found so much peace and consolation. She wondered if she now was approaching the criteria for clinical depression, and so on top of the anger and sadness, she was scared.

"How could anyone let this happen for so many years?" she demanded. "I just can't believe nobody stopped it."

Sadly, as a survivor of family abuse, I know exactly how this kind of thing happened. I was totally unsurprised by all the cover-ups, because I have seen that dynamic at work in my family of origin: Adults "protect" adults from kids who tell the truth. The adults escape justice. The kids are left in chains that only grow tighter with age unless those chains are deliberately broken by the very person who suffers them.

At this point, I looked at Marissa and wondered, given the types of people who'd surrounded me for most of my life, if I might be in the presence of some sort of unicorn.

I asked, "You've *never* lived with a family secret?"

She shook her head once, adamantly. "No!"

Her voice was justly thick with revulsion. I recognized the sound. She was feeling the same disgust and rage I'd wrestled with ever since coming to terms with the fact that my chains were *real*, that I *had* survived child abuse and neglect, that I was the only one who had ever tried to stop it, and that I seemed to be the only one suffering for it thus far.

On the one hand, having grown up with my own experience of family, I was grateful my friend had been spared the kind of pain that I just take for granted as part of so many people's lives. On the other hand, it was hard to imagine growing up in a world where the roots of adult-child relationships weren't rotten through with secrets that were not surprises, with adults protecting adults from justice at the sacrifice of children.

Because her voice now was an echo of my own, I felt the Lord leading me to share with her the one thing that has helped me to see that God was on my side, on the side of all the abused, all along, even though — *especially because* — that abuse was permitted through God's gift of free will.

I asked, "Do you think for one second that you are angrier than God is that this happened?"

I watched her jaw drop. She was speechless for a moment before she replied, "I hadn't thought of it that way. I guess I don't see God as angry."

"Of course he gets angry! He hates sin. He especially hates sin against innocent children." I went on, describing the lesson I have learned in my own healing. "The rage you feel at this is just a thin shadow of the rage God feels at seeing his children behave this way. If you think you are angrier than God is about this, then you don't know God."

Once she'd composed herself, she gave me a gift, a healing gift, a gift that placed a jewel on all the healing work I've striven to do with God's help.

"Thank you," she said. "That is the first thing that anyone's said about this that's made any sense."

Just Following Order

Once again, Jesus is no dummy. If we cherry-pick this Beatitude from its place following the blessings on the teachable, the emotionally connected, and on those who honor boundaries, a "hunger and thirst for justice" sounds like a call to vengeful arms. That, of course, would contradict the God who first gave us the verse in Deuteronomy, quoted at the head of this chapter, laying a boundary around vengeance, claiming and keeping it as his own. Jesus put this Beatitude in this order because he wants this desire to be rightly ordered before we look to him to satisfy it — so that we can look to him and not ourselves to satisfy it.

So what is that right order? When we experience and practice confidence in a truly loving God, we see with compassion every sinful human we meet. We want to share the compassion God has lovingly lavished upon us. In that compassion, we see our own need for his guidance, and we let our spirits become poor, needy — teachable. Once we are ready to learn, we can learn from the emotions God gave to us and to those upon whom he asks us to have compassion, no matter how they act.

If we become students of those emotions rather than slaves to them, we are then in a position to honor where our responsibility toward those emotions begins and ends: We surrender our desire to overpower, cajole, or otherwise control. Instead we seek to honor boundaries: others, ours, and God's. Once that desire to control is surrendered, our consciences are free, no longer dominated by our whims or the whims of others who may still want to control us. A conscience thus sensitized will convey to us accurate information regarding our own temptations so that we can avoid hurting God and others. A sensitive conscience likewise calls us to courageous responsibility in those times when we do fail.

That said, once we see the damage that comes from boundary violations, the Beatitudes now recirculate: A sensitive conscience empowers us to see the damage caused by all violations against the boundaries of human dignity — all offenses against meekness. Because we know the value of comfort for mourning, we honor the pain those violations have caused. We want ourselves and others — sinners of all stripes — to be teachable enough to stop causing such pain because it stings our now-compassionate hearts, which in turn sting for the compassionate heart of a loving God. We want to stand up for our truly loving Father, the one in heaven, the one we love through self-love and love of neighbor, because he first loved us.

Of course, we cycle-breakers have experienced the disruption of God's order from our very earliest days. We were taught injustice by the very people tasked with teaching us right from wrong. Humans taught us to carry burdens that weren't ours in order to give adults a false buffer from the results of their wrongs. We were taught to ignore the emotions that threatened to awaken the dulled consciences of those who hurt us. We learned that the only way to be "safe" is to dig in our heels and be perfect — or fake it as well as we can and lash back at anyone who suggests otherwise. We became unteachable.

In short, we have been traumatized. Doesn't God see what happened to us? Doesn't he care? How can we teach our children mercy and compassion when we've experienced so little of it ourselves *and* it looks like God doesn't punish child abusers? If he let our parents get away with it, then what's to stop us? Where is this righteousness we now so desperately crave?

Whether in our relationships with our families of origin, with our own children, or really with any other human in our circles, specific spiritual pitfalls lie between childhood trauma survivors and the true satisfaction this Beatitude offers. We are liable to believe false ideas of justice, mercy, anger, and retribution. We are at risk of living those false ideas out upon our children. We are at risk of buying these lies should our unrepentant parents try to keep selling them to us. We are at risk of using those false ideas to usurp

God's vengeance and pour it out upon our families of origin — and upon our helpless children.

Thankfully, in this Beatitude, God carries us over those pitfalls. He offers us consolation for the sins committed against him and us. He sensitizes us to right and wrong. He frees us to act in accordance with a newly formed and sharpened conscience. Through all of this, he uses us to right the wrongs that were visited upon us as helpless children, offering our unrepentant parents the opportunity to get right with him before it's too late. Best of all, through paying heed to our awakened consciences, we make room for him to make all things new for the next generation and beyond.

A sharp conscience is a healthy conscience is a joyful conscience. All we have to do is keep surrendering ourselves to him. It's that simple. It's that difficult.

Consolation Prizes

I am coming up against a bit of a translation issue here. The New American Bible, Revised Edition, the translation used in liturgy in the United States, translates this Beatitude as a hunger and thirst for "righteousness," while the Douay-Rheims (an older Catholic translation) describes a hunger and thirst for "justice." For the purposes of continuity, I've been using the newer translation thus far. But for this particular Beatitude, in this context of healing for survivors of family abuse and dysfunction, I'd like to look more specifically at the word *justice*.

While righteousness and justice are essentially the same thing — a realization of how things are supposed to be — in today's language, righteousness has been poisoned by connotations with "self-righteousness," or a blindness to one's own sins and an eagerness to punish others' for theirs. This is the type of parenting that most of us are struggling against having survived, fighting not to follow this flawed way in our own choices with our own children. Also, many of us have been denied justice for the sins our unrepentant parents committed against us, and they have defended their perceived right to commit those sins. Thus it seems more helpful to discuss this as a hunger and thirst for *justice*.

Justice, however, has its own connotations of vengeance and retribution. This presents several complications for adults who are striving for holiness after being parented themselves without the boundaries provided by our recently discussed Beatitude of meekness. Most of our parents sought to control rather than to love us, and any hint that they were treating us with injustice was likely to be met with denial at best, enraged retribution at worst. In order to keep their flawed perception of control over us, they felt compelled to deny our very holy hunger for justice, a hunger intrinsic to a humanity created in the image and likeness of a just and merciful God.

I know so much of the previous chapters have been dedicated to making the case that a loving God cares about the pain you've experienced. I also know, through my own pain, that this can be a hard case to make. That's why I want to make sure you see God's care through each Beatitude, including this one — *especially* this one. I know how your confidence in God's love for you might falter because I still feel mine falter on an almost daily basis. This is why I want to talk to you now, in terms of justice, about any anger you may have at your parents' sins. Just like I told my friend Marissa (and just like I have to tell the face in the mirror every day), our anger at sin is a mere shadow of God's. He lets us feel that anger because he wants to share his whole heart with us so that we can feel safe enough, through relationship, to share our whole hearts with him. God is bigger than our biggest emotions.

But what do you do if you aren't even convinced that your pain is a heart-cry for justice against actual sin, that you didn't just make this up so you could live out some victim-fantasy against your poor parents? The survivor of family abuse and dysfunction has been raised to question the reality of his feelings and experiences. Thus you may still be struggling with some doubt that you were, in fact, the victim of your parent's sin. Isn't thinking of your parents as sinners an offense against the commandment to honor your father and mother? Thankfully, those of us whose mothers and fathers have been less than holy have none other than Pope Saint John Paul II to show us the truth. In *Familiaris Consortio*, he points out that a family isn't supposed to alienate each other through selfishness. Rather, he says, "All members of the family, each according to his or her own gift, have the grace and responsibility of building, day by day, the communion of persons … this happens where there is care and love for the little ones, the sick, the aged; where there is mutual service every day; when there is a sharing of goods, of joys and of sorrows."[32]

What happens to the family that does not see each other in terms of mutual service? "Without love the family is not a community of persons and, in the same way, without love the family cannot live, grow and perfect itself as a community of persons."[33] Through *Familiaris Consortio*, God reminds us that hunger for love, affection, belonging are all signs of a hunger for justice. The desire for our parents to fulfill this responsibility of family is right and just.

By God himself through the Church, our pain is explained and justified. We don't need to defend it to families of origin who want our pain to disappear without the hard work of bringing themselves to justice. Further, wanting our sinful parents to have consequences for their sins is part of our humanity, part of our role as bearers of the image and likeness of God. God wants them to face their reality as well. He makes this clear throughout his word. Yes, Jesus speaks of mercy, but he speaks of mercy to the *repentant*, not to those entrenched in their sin. For those who refuse to repent, God makes clear what waits for them, and it's not pretty. If you want reassurance

32. John Paul II, *Familiaris Consortio*, par. 21..
33 Ibid., par. 18.

on that, go check out Galatians 6:7, Luke 13:1–5, and Acts 3:19. In each of these verses and many more, God promises us mercy if we repent, but death if we do not.[34]

Still tempted to tell yourself that your parents didn't know any better than to hurt you? Perhaps they have personality disorders. Perhaps they were abused themselves and don't know any better. Let me assure you: If you ever cried out in any kind of pain from their unjust treatment, they know. Denial may not be an actual river, but a person can still drown in it. They know. Their sins are their fault and not your responsibility to erase or absolve. Once they know their sin, they are subject to God's word. In Acts 3, God through Peter addressed people who had Christ put to death, reminding them that they "acted out of ignorance." Ignorance, however, does not absolve them because God fulfilled his promises in Christ's suffering and resurrection; Christ's murderers now have seen the truth and, if they actually do want their sins wiped away, they are bound to repentance (see Acts 3:17–19).

We want justice because God wants justice. God's heart breaks for the traumatized child you were, maybe still are, and he yearns to make sure you see not mere human justice, but *his* justice. He has enticed your conscience to wake up in his loving presence so that you will neither ignore the injustices inflicted against you or others, nor will you try to inflict upon your persecutors a justice of your making. Through relationship with God the Father, we receive not a cheap vengeance but the consolation of knowing that, no matter how big our hurt is, God is bigger. He has way more power than we do to make things right for good.

Knowing that God aches when his children hurt each other doesn't just console us in our own experience as adult children, but also in our experience as parents. Here's a harsh fact for the

---

34. While this reality — that God's mercy is poured out freely but only for the repentant — is everywhere in the Bible for those with eyes to see, my eyes were first opened to this by Luke 17:3 Ministries (http://www.luke173ministries.org).

perfectionists among us: Even if we threw off every single shackle of wrongly spirited parenting we learned growing up, repented perfectly, and never again made a single parenting mistake of our own, we'd still be raising sinners. Our own kids are going to hurt us, sometimes multiple times a day, sometimes in reaction to our sins against them, and sometimes just because, well, they're humans with free will and are free to make bad choices.

Humans sin. It happens. So how is it a consolation to know that God is upset at our kids' sins too? Under the influence of a dulled conscience, that knowledge could be used to violate meekness with spiritual abuse. Spiritual abuse happens when we put ourselves in place of God and ruthlessly punish our children for what they've done wrong. In case it's not obvious, this is a violation of meekness and especially of God's role as judge.

Thankfully, Jesus put this Beatitude after those that invite us to be teachable, emotionally connected, and respectful of boundaries. When we place our desire for justice with our children in context of God's dominion over all justice, we are set free to connect with our kids before we correct them. We see this parenting gig not as an opportunity to unleash God's wrath upon anyone. Our job, rather, is to live Ephesians 6:4, which says, "Do not provoke your children to anger, but bring them up with the training and instruction of the Lord."

If God can console us in our parents' unrepentance, of course God will console us for whatever pain our children's sins might bring us. Once we believe that God will handle justice rightly, we don't need to make anyone hurt as much as they've hurt us, especially our children. Because we now know God cares about all of us sinners, we know he longs for all of us to repent and turn back to true relationship with him. He aches when we don't. As much as sin might bother us, nobody wants things made right more than he does. Knowing God is in control, between our parents' sins, our children's, and most of all our own, at last we can rest satisfied in

God's righteous care for all souls.

What's Next? Me First
A couple of unexpected things happen when you discover that
God is on your side and has been all along, even through your parents' sins. First, you realize that your biggest ally is the biggest force
for justice in this universe or any other. Next, as a result of that
consolation, you can feel safer. I mean, you've got this omniscient,
omnipotent person who wants good things for you for eternity.
Who wouldn't loosen up a bit, right? Now that you're relaxing,
though, you start to look around a bit, think your own thoughts,
compare what you've lived to what God wants for you and all his
children ... and that's when you realize that being on God's side
now means you are aware of exactly how bad things were.

And now that we realize how bad things were, our eyes open up
to how bad we have made it for others sometimes. Those boundaries we learned about with meekness? We see them violated all over
the place, including by us. That emotional connection we discovered with mourning? We are resensitized to how that was denied us,
but we also see clearly how we have denied others that connection.
We're finally open to learning those lessons that we can only grasp
through poverty of spirit, and we see at last how very many people
we have hurt in our stubbornness. There will be times, now that you
are really living the depth of your hunger for God's justice, that it
will all seem too much for one human to handle.

It is too much for any human to handle. God knows that, and
he equips us for that reality in Matthew 7:1–5, those verses discussed earlier about the planks in our own eyes and the splinters
in our brother's.

So often, these verses are used as an affront to meekness, as
a violation of boundaries, as a tool to shut up the corrector who
points out another's injustice. I mean, how many of us, expressing
our pain to unrepentant parents, have heard in response, "Don't

you judge me!" If we look at what this Scripture is saying to one with a healthy conscience, however, we see something entirely different. We see an invitation to connect to God, self, and others with sensitivity. It takes a lot of numbness, after all, to ignore anything in one's own eye, much less an entire wooden beam!

Take King David, who was willing to have his conscience re-sensitized even after a series of massive sins. He was responsible for the rape of a woman and, when she fell pregnant as a result, the murder of her husband. He should have been destroyed, just as King Saul before him. Not so David, however. Why not? In 2 Samuel 12, the prophet Nathan clearly shows David the depravity of his actions. Where Saul, confronted with his sin, denied and justified his actions, David learns from Nathan, acknowledges his sin, and repents. He comes clean with the truth. He asks God's mercy, but he accepts the punishment meted out for him. In Psalm 26, David even writes a prayer, begging God, "Judge me, Lord!"

When we truly fear the Lord as even David did, we live the fruit of this Beatitude, to hunger and thirst for justice. Rightly lived, this Beatitude leads us to hunger and thirst that justice will be served to us first. We know that justice is only served if we repent of any injustices we commit, if we first remove the planks from our own eyes. Not only does this rescue us from all the dangers of hypocrisy, but as survivors of family abuse and dysfunction, seeking justice against ourselves first turns us into the opposite of what our parents were to us. They sought to remain unteachable, to reshape reality through emotional dominance, to erase their sins by pretending their sins don't exist. Like Adam and Eve, they thought they could hide their shame. Rather, Jesus warns us that, eventually, all secrets will be laid bare, and there will be no more hiding (see Lk 12:2).

How does this play out in our family relationships today? A conscience sensitive to injustice will stop normalizing any ongoing abuse from unrepentant parents. If your parents try to blame-shift, gaslight, belittle or otherwise abuse you, you're now free to recognize it's wrong and tell them so, even if they have their hearts set on staying unrepentant. If you see them do anything unkind toward your children, you'll really be free to recognize their sin for what it is and stand up for your children's boundaries, even to the point of ending contact with your parents, if need be (more on that in the next chapter).

As for the relationship between you and your children, your hunger and thirst for righteousness will make sure you feel that plank in your own eye well before you try taking any specks from theirs. This is God's protection over your parenting, so that you can see clearly to help your child grow in righteousness. Your sharpened conscience will show you when to apologize to your kids so that they know you're not some domineering monster with whom no relationship is possible. Instead they'll know you're just a fellow sinner, if one with authority to correct and guide them, and you're both just walking together on the path that leads to eternal life. This togetherness will be handy for those times when you do need to correct them, first because you'll have credibility, and second because you'll be much less likely to lash out in violation of meekness.

All of this is because a sensitive conscience is like a small, stubborn dog who insists on being at your heels while you're cooking. Once your conscience is aligned with God's justice, if you try to ignore it, it won't let you. Thank God!

Simply Sated

My friend Marissa from the beginning of the chapter, and every single person who is angry about child abuse — abuse of any kind, really — have been given a gift directly from the Lord himself. That gift is this Beatitude: a hunger and thirst for what is good. That gift will be heavy to carry at times, but it is heavy like a suit of armor in that it protects us from irrevocably destroying our relationship with God and those he's given us to love. It places a protective layer around the blessings all the other Beatitudes provide. That gift is a sensitive conscience. A sensitive conscience is key to living joyfully, especially with our children — and with our families of origin — as God makes all things new through us.

It bears repeating: God hurts when we hurt. In his just mercy, he will take care of those who hurt us. Of course, there's the reality that sometimes we are the ones doing the hurting. He will take care of us, too. Knowing that God aches when his children hurt each other empowers our consciences to guide us through our own parenting choices. This knowledge also frees us to respond to our parents with loving truth, even if they yet remain unrepentant.

This Beatitude promises us satisfaction for our hunger and thirst for all justice, not just justice for our own choices. Further, the Beatitude "Blessed are those who mourn" taught us that others' sins against us do deserve legitimate redress. So now that our consciences have been reset to recognize sins from us and against us, how are we to handle spiritually immature people who do us wrong? In case you were wondering, I chose the phrase "spiritually immature people" deliberately because that can apply to both our parents and our children. The former are spiritually immature and often choose to stay that way; the latter are spiritually immature because God created us to grow in wisdom before him and humans, especially those humans tasked with raising them.

This is where mercy will come in. This is why Jesus acknowledges the validity of our hunger and thirst for justice first, before he promises us his divine mercy for our own human mercy. As with all things in the dysfunctional family, however, you may be carrying a great deal of baggage around the very word "mercy." Those who lack poverty of spirit are known to act as if mercy is owed them freely without a need to repent. Those who lack emotional connection or boundaries are prone to demanding mercy as a way to obliterate any discomfort empathy might cause them. Thus mercy may have been poisoned in your head until it looks more like enabling others to continue in sin without consequence. As we see in this Beatitude, however, Jesus will not let the unrepentant continue in sin forever. Such is not the nature of truth.

True mercy, the mercy that flows from the wounded side of Christ, is the choice made by a person who forgives toward the person who repents. It is a rebuilding of a relationship where both people now want what is true to last between them. Mercy flows upon the repentant heart because Jesus always desires our return. He is, after all, the one who created the rupture/repair cycle, and that is where we can feel the beat of his merciful heart doing its salvific work. This is the mercy we practice when we approach our own sins and the inevitable sins of our children with rupture/repair in mind rather than control and appeasement.

We can starve to death and we can die of thirst in this life, but if we continue to hunger and thirst for what is right at the cost of all other longings, we will be satisfied. Our parents' sins against us were wrong and not our fault. There is nothing wrong with wanting them to face consequences for their actions. Our sins against our children are not their fault. There is everything good about asking Jesus to help us face our consequences. Our children's sins are not our fault, and Jesus asks us to show them by word and deed how to repent. Jesus asks us, in the nagging of our consciences, to trust in his complete and perfect wisdom. In our next Beatitude, he shows us how to do just that.

HOLY FAMILY MOMENT:
"Blessed Are Those Who Hear the Word of God and Observe It."
(Lk 11:27–28)

When a woman shouted to him that the womb that bore him and the breasts that nursed him were blessed, Jesus' response, "Rather, blessed are those who hear the word of God and observe it," might seem dismissive. Really, he was acknowledging that just having a child doesn't win you any prizes or justify any of your mistakes. Jesus knows that a womb that bears and breasts that nurse can be in the same body as a heart that betrays the fruit of that love. Perfection is not assured just because you have children with a duty to honor you. Discovering the true meaning of justice and acting on that meaning — including proper repentance when we go astray — is the real blessing in all our family relationships.

BEATITUDE BASIC WORKSHOP
Sensitivity of Conscience

1. *Memento mori* is Latin for "Remember your death." In your journal, write a prayer, asking God to give you the strength and wisdom to remember that judgment before him is your unavoidable destiny, not to mention your children's. Include a prayer for your parents, living or dead, from whom you've never seen any sign of repentance, and ask God to encourage them to face all truth, for that is the only way to face him.

2. If you don't already, mark your calendar with a monthly commitment to receive the Sacrament of Reconciliation. Frequent confession keeps your conscience sharp and protects you and those around you from sin.

3. Spend time journaling over the following Scriptures

regarding God's idea of justice: Ps 7:13, Prov 16:5, Gal 6:7, Rom 1:18, Rom 2:5–8, 2 Pt 2:9. Look into and develop the practice of *lectio divina* (divine reading), so that you can hear God's voice and actively entrust justice in your life to his care.

NUNC DIMITTIS (LK 2:29–32)
Now, Master, you may let your servant go
   in peace, according to your word,
for my eyes have seen your salvation,
   which you prepared in sight of all the peoples,
a light for revelation to the Gentiles,
   and glory for your people Israel.

SAINT-SPIRATION
Saint Martin de Porres

If ever there were a saint who knew both hunger and thirst of both the material and the spiritual kind, it would have to be Saint Martin de Porres. The child of a formerly enslaved mother and a European father, Martin grew up in the boomtown of Lima, Peru. When his father abandoned the family, his mother blamed Martin for the loss and subjected the little boy to beatings, beratings, and a roster of chores too heavy for even a well-provided-for boy of eight — which Martin most certainly was not, so impoverished were they by the loss of his father's presence and income. It would be another four years before his father would provide any assistance to his "mixed" family, and even then it was only to secure Martin an apprenticeship with a barber-surgeon.

Grace builds on nature. By all reports, Martin had always been kind to all creatures, both human and otherwise, but perhaps his firsthand experience with deprivation kept charity foremost in his heart. He became a Dominican brother and performed the monastery's most menial labor with joy. He first rescued animals from destruction, but as time went on, he grew into rescuing children, too, finding and building homes for abandoned children of all sorts. He hungered for justice in his world and brought it to life through charity.[35]

---

35. Dominican Sisters of Saint Cecelia, "Saint Martin de Porres," accessed February 16, 2021, https://www.nashvilledominican.org/community/our-dominican-heritage/our-saints-and-blesseds/st-martin-de-porres/.

– 7 –

BLESSED ARE THE
MERCIFUL

For They Will Be Shown Mercy

Beatitude Basic: Repentance

O L*ORD, our God, you answered them;*
you were a forgiving God to them,
though you punished their offenses.

— Psalm 99:8

An Infestation

It was the very start of yet another hot, humid Pennsylvania summer. It was exactly the kind of weather for a teenager to have some friends over to celebrate the end of the school year. Unfortunately, it also was exactly the kind of weather that makes fleas thrive on family pets, even indoor ones like my very large and lazy cat, Hobie. Hobie was my cat — certainly not the family cat, my father made that very clear — and thus I was the one to blame for the flea problem. My father spent a lot of the money he earned at the job he hated on flea dips for my cat and flea bombs for his house. He made it clear that this suffering was all my fault, and that I wasn't allowed to have friends over until I had gotten rid of the fleas. I'd made the mistake of asking if we could at least just hang out outside. My request was met with an unloading of my father's rage.

I remember sitting on the concrete steps just outside our front door, letting his fury wash over me, knowing it would quiet down eventually, knowing that I would get the silent treatment soon enough. I just had to white-knuckle my way through yet another scream-fest. Silence was unpleasant, sure, but far less unpleasant than his yelling about how I was ruining his house, and how I seemed to care more about my friends than about his house.

When he finally paused to refill his lungs, I remember saying quietly, "I love my friends."

I did not see his face when he replied, "Well, I love my house."

Sitting on those steps, I remember thinking, *Surely he doesn't love his house more than people, does he? He's just saying that to punish me for having a cat who keeps getting fleas. Why did I say anything at all, anyway? A good child accepts all the punishment a parent gives and doesn't challenge it. A good child wouldn't have a cat with fleas either.*

The screaming lowered in volume, but the rant continued. I distinctly remember hearing my father say to my back, "I don't understand what your problem is. *I'm not some kind of monster.*"

I wondered, if he really wasn't a monster, then why did he so regularly rage like one? Of course, I had the sense to keep this sentiment to myself, which probably went a long way toward making that rage die down back to its usual silent simmer. As I look back on this story, I wonder why I felt so led to share it in the opening of the chapter on mercy. Clearly there was no mercy here. The parent showed raging control, not mercy. An argument could be made that teenage me showed mercy in not matching rage for rage, but that did not win me any mercy in return. Then again, what does mercy even look like? Is it a transactional form of peace that says, "If I'm nice to you, you have to be nice to me?" Or is it something deeper, more stable and available because its source is a loving God, not fallen humans?

Spoilers: Mercy is deeper. Mercy is relational, undeserved, not transactional. All the Beatitudes before this one deliver mercy into our hearts not so we can turn a blind eye to sin, but so we can look anyone's sin straight in the eye and respond with teachability and emotional connection balanced with good boundaries and a solid sense of right and wrong. Like a disordered definition of meekness, mercy is misunderstood as being a doormat. Mercy honors the boundaries God gives us so that we surrender judgment to him. Then, being aware of both God's power to judge and his mercy to redeem, we will do anything in our powerlessness to repent of our sins and be a part of God's healing work.

This Beatitude tells us that a child who is merciful to a parent like this will be shown mercy. This Beatitude also promises mercy to the parent who shows mercy to his child. We might miss the fact that the source of that mercy is God, not our parents or anyone else for that matter. On top of that, survivors of family abuse and dysfunction did not grow up with much real mercy. How can we then model mercy for our own children? Perhaps more importantly, how can we model mercy for ourselves, with our own newly sensitive consciences cheerfully pointing out to us the things we've done wrong?

So what is mercy? Mercy is that quality of God that says, "I know how hard it is to be holy. All I ask you to do is be honest about that." That honesty, with God, self, and others, is better known as repentance. In order for us survivors of family abuse and dysfunction to unravel the mystery that is Christlike mercy, accessed by repentance, we would do well first to examine the mechanism that prevents parents like my father — and, often enough, like me — from showing mercy.

War Is Hell (Because Sin Is, Too)

Years ago, I met my friend Jenna* through a women's ministry program. On retreat, she talked about how her father had served in Vietnam, and that, according to her mother, he had come home *changed*. Jenna wouldn't know, however. She never knew her father before the war. Her memory was of her father as an angry man and a hard drinker. Jenna is one of a handful of friends who tell a similar tale: a nice man who went to war but came back mean, and his children never knew him as anything but abusive.

It's very easy for us to blame an infection of rage into a person's psyche on Post-Traumatic Stress Disorder (PTSD), a collection of symptoms and behaviors that can affect a person who has survived a traumatic event, anything from a mugging to a devastating hurricane to outright war, or even that tornado we talked about in the chapter on meekness. PTSD, however, is a way for us to understand what happens to a person who has been *victimized* by circumstances beyond his control. More recently, however, I've started seeing some mention of veterans suffering something called "moral injury" as opposed to plain old PTSD.

Authors Rita Nakashima Brock and Gabriella Lettini are two women who, like my friend Jenna, were raised by men whose experiences in war affected their later ability to parent healthily. Together they wrote *Soul Repair: Recovering from Moral Injury After War* about this reality and the experience of moral injury. In *Soul Repair*, they elaborate on the post-war effects of moral injury in soldiers, saying,

> Moral injury results when [in war] soldiers violate their
> core moral beliefs and in evaluating their behavior neg-

atively, they feel they no longer live in a reliable, mean-
ingful world and can no longer be regarded as decent
human beings. They may feel this even if what they did
was warranted and unavoidable.

> The consequences of violating one's conscience,
> even if the act was unavoidable or seemed right at the
> time, can be devastating. Responses include overwhelm-
> ing depression, guilt, and self-medication through
> alcohol or drugs ... Connecting emotionally to others
> becomes impossible for those trapped inside the walls of
> such feelings.[36]

Moral injury, then, is a term that describes the mental landscape
not necessarily of the victim but of the perpetrator. Soldiers were
victims when bullets flew their way, but they also sent bullets of
their own coursing toward other soldiers just like them. Victims
aren't the only ones affected by violence. PTSD describes how a
psyche may act when it has been battered by circumstances out
of its control. Moral injury describes how a psyche is affected
when pain is a result of the person's own choices and actions.
What's amazing to me is that PTSD and moral injury have many
of the same manifestations: depression, irritability, violence, ad-
dictive behaviors, hopelessness, suicidal thoughts and actions.

I'm no expert, but this tells me that, for all the power it
seems our parents may have had over us in their abuse, the way
they wielded that power hurt them terribly. If they remained unteachable, they refused the lessons their mistakes offered. They
denied our emotions in order to falsely soothe their own. Turns
out that was a bad bargain. It was a bad bargain for which we
ourselves do not want to fall.

---

36. Rita Nakashima Brock and Gabriella Lettini, *Soul Repair: Recovering from Moral Injury After War* (Boston: Beacon Press, 2012), xv–xvi.

Some Kind of Monster

Any survivors who know their Bible will not be at all surprised by the idea of moral injury. It is perhaps an older pain than even PTSD. The first sin committed was not human against human (Cain took care of that a bit later). The first sin, rather, was against the self and the very heart of right relationship with a loving God. This may be an unpopular opinion, but the main reason abusers abuse is *not* because they are acting out their own abuse. Otherwise, where would the first sin have come from? God is perfect and the parent of our first parents, Adam and Eve, who sinned without being taught how. No, abuse begins with loneliness — the unique loneliness that sorely tempts us to sin because somehow we think that God won't fill us up when the people who are supposed to love us leave us behind.

I'm no theologian, so this theory may be off base; but for the sake of argument, let's say Eve was alone when the serpent found her. Where was Adam? Wasn't it not good for the man to be alone? So already we have some "not good" starting, and that's where the serpent found his chance — in Eve's loneliness. Now, leaving someone alone isn't necessarily a sin, but abandoning those we are called to love and serve leaves the door open for sin, and Jesus is pretty clear about what happens to people who don't protect others from sin: "Things that cause sin will inevitably occur, but woe to the person through whom they occur. It would be better for him if a millstone were put around his neck and he be thrown into the sea than for him to cause one of these little ones to sin" (Lk 17:1–2).

So looking for a balm to her loneliness, Eve sinned. The problem is that sin only made her more lonely. She was a creature of the only species on earth capable of having a relationship with God, and she was now the only person on earth who had disregarded that relationship. She had made herself infinitely more lonely. She had exiled herself from relationship. And God said it's not good for us to be alone. Rather than repenting of her sin, she asked Adam to join her. To their horror, they were not any less lonely. Rather, they were more lonely than before only Eve had sinned. They even asked each other to look away until they could cover up their naked reality. So what did Adam and Eve do when God confronted them about their sin? Did they admit their vulnerability and ask forgiveness? Of course not. They blame-shifted.

"The person you stuck me with made me do it!"

"I was tricked into hurting you!"

"I couldn't help myself!"

"It was the best I could do!"

Sound familiar? Probably the only reason they didn't say, "You're making a big deal out of nothing, God," is because humans were only just getting started on sin. They hadn't yet developed all the sick tools of denial.

Adam and Eve, like we all tend to do, thought they could cover up the pain of sin with yet more sin. They, obviously, were wrong. This pattern repeats itself age upon age, in soul upon soul. Our developing understanding of moral injury, however, brings surprising new insight into why people are so good at hiding from sin and so bad at repairing it. Brock and Lettini even describe this in *Soul Repair*:

> By eating of that forbidden tree, [Adam and Eve] wanted knowledge they could not handle, like young soldiers who go to war imagining it as a personal test of their prowess, a video game, or a movie. When their eyes are opened by the knowledge they sought, Adam and Eve realize ... try to hide from the consequences .... They have failed the test of moral discernment and responsibility. They are cursed with enmity and hardship ... To prohibit their return to the Garden, an angel with a flaming sword guards the gate. Outside that gate are fratricide, war, empire, slavery, misogyny, and myriad forces of

oppression. When we violate our core moral values and fail to take responsibility, our moral conscience takes up that fierce flaming sword and guards what is left of our moral identity. To reenter the Garden, humanity must face that fierce angel.[37]

In order to repair the damage incurred on the soul by the soul's own sin, one must return to God and his original plan for our well-being, which was obedience to him and a manifestation of his care in our relationships with our fellow humans. We must face the reality our sin has created. We must face the very flaming sword that terrifies us: our own failings against conscience. This is the very heart of the upward climb that is repentance. If one has not grown in love of God, love of neighbor and self, teachability, emotional connection, healthy boundaries, and sensitivity of conscience, repentance is all but impossible. The cycle of sin, especially family sin, continues unchecked.

This is why I'm reasonably confident that the main reason abusers abuse is *not* because they are acting out their own abuse. They're just hiding from the pain they feel when they realize what their own sinful choices have done to their relationship with themselves. If they hide themselves from those people they are called to serve, they don't have to look at themselves as the monsters they've let themselves become.

When I first started reading about moral injury, I heard that memory of my father saying, "I'm not some kind of monster." As a child, dependent on him, when he would say that sort of thing, I thought what he probably wanted me to think: my fear of him was unwarranted and I was being unfair to him. As an adult, however, I realized that he was saying that to convince *himself*, because somewhere deep inside of himself, he knew his behavior was not compatible with his idea of what a good father should be. I have no

---

37. Nakashima Brock and Lettini, *Soul Repair*, 127.

doubt that he suffered emotional neglect at the hands of his own parents, which probably caused him some level of PTSD, with the attendant symptoms of irritability and verbal violence. Because of his lack of spiritual poverty, his lack of teachability, he refused to see that he needed to change. Thus he disconnected himself from the painful emotions he found in my reactions to his sin. Then he tried forcing me to change my emotions to better suit his comfort, thus violating my boundaries and the virtue of meekness. He denied my hunger and thirst to be treated with justice and, in doing so, denied the reality of God's inevitable justice. Through his rage, he incurred on himself a state of moral injury, and in the ensuing layers of hopelessness, he impaired his ability to offer his children mercy. To admit his own need of mercy would be to admit the habit of sin he was too afraid to face.

Moral injury, then, describes for us why people tend away from repentance, why we humans are so afraid of letting God make us new. What does that have to do with how we show mercy? If we are to approach our parents, our children, and ourselves with true mercy we need to know and understand the landscape of tendencies that make up fallen human relationships. We also need to know how to, as Christ says in Luke 6:36, "Be merciful, just as [also] your Father is merciful." That sounds like a tall order. That sounds like we need to become doormats and let people abuse us, let our children run rampant without ever having to suffer our parental correction, let ourselves suffer the same hurts over and over again from the generations that sandwich us.

Allow God's word to reassure you: Your Father is merciful in a way that frees you from habitual abuse by your family of origin. God is merciful, unendingly merciful. God, however, isn't indiscriminately merciful. "Forgive and forget" is not in the Bible.

Under One Condition

Don't misunderstand me: God is eager to tell us about his mercy and just as excited to share that mercy with us. There isn't a single book in the Bible that doesn't at least allude to God's mercy and rescue. Psalm 103 is a lovely, heartening description of God's mercy. In verses 11–12, we read, "For as the heavens tower over the earth, so his mercy towers over those who fear him. As far as the east is from the west, so far has he removed our sins from us." It is vitally important for us to read the next verse, however: "As a father has compassion on his children, *so the Lord has compassion on those who fear him.*" For those of us with earthly fathers who resoundingly failed at the practice of compassion, this verse carries a dark weight. However, this verse describes earthly fathers who *do* have compassion. This verse also tells us that God's compassion is infinite, but he only shares that compassion with those who know and value his personality, his goodness, his righteousness, and our unworthiness in comparison.

When it comes to mercy, God's personality is no different in the New Testament. In Luke 19:1–10, we read the story of the scheming Zacchaeus, upon whom Jesus freely poured mercy in this life — but only after Zacchaeus changed his ways and strove to repair the damage he had done to his enemies. In the Parable of the Prodigal Son, Jesus tells us of a father who welcomes his son back with open arms only after that son *first in his mind and then in his actions* turns back home and says, "Father, I have sinned against heaven and against you; I no longer deserve to be called your son" (Lk 15:21). Even when we hear the Parable of the Lost Sheep (Mt 18:10–14), where the shepherd goes after a single sheep who got himself lost, we must consider it in the context of Jesus calling himself the Good Shepherd (see Jn 10:1–16). Jesus tells us the Good Shepherd lays down his life for his sheep, but he also says that those sheep can only be saved by entering through him, by knowing his voice and being known by him. Repentance brings us into his fold, but if we do not repent, we are not his sheep. We are the thorns and briers that imprison the lost.

Of course, it's not God's desire for any of us to be lost, even the worst child abuser. He gives us chance after chance. He tells us plainly in Luke 13 that death comes for all of us, sometimes through our own choices, sometimes through accident, but it is unavoidable. In the Parable of the Barren Fig Tree (Lk 13:6–9), he gives us a very clear image of his desire that we choose the temporary pain of repentance over the eternal pain of death. In this parable, Jesus talks of a landowner who wanted a barren fig tree ripped out. The gardener pleaded with the owner to give him one more year to work on the tree, in hopes that it would turn that care to fruitfulness. The owner and gardener agree that the tree will be given a limited time to improve — a clear boundary. If it does not improve, then it must be torn out. We have chances to repent, but only within the finite window of whatever lifespan God wishes to grant us, and only he knows the width of that window.

Jesus gives us a very plain road map to making the most of that window, however wide it may or may not be. He puts blessings on the merciful after blessings on the teachable, the emotionally connected, the meek, and those who listen to well-formed consciences. This is natural. It's hard not to see ourselves and others with mercy once we're willing to learn from God's heart, acknowledge the truth of our and others' feelings, respect the differences between what is rightfully theirs and ours, and act from a confident awareness of right and wrong. We naturally become merciful toward all, especially ourselves, as we practice the Beatitudes that led into this one. How? Our consciences teach us, the newly teachable, how weak and sinful we can be, exactly how prone we are to violating boundaries and railroading over any emotions that get in our way.

We see our need for change. In trying to change, we see how hard change is. That is the heart of becoming merciful as the Father is merciful. God knows how hard we have it because not only did he ordain our hardships as our teaching moments, but he also had his own hardships to endure, up to and including the most painful death humankind has ever devised: death on a cross. We can be merciful to ourselves now because we know how hard it is to be holy. We can be merciful to our children in ways we never received from our parents because we are aware now of how inescapably hard it is to be a human. We can even be merciful to our parents because we either know or can imagine how terrifying it is to live with moral injury, that traumatization of self and others that only God can heal.

We can heal through letting all the Beatitudes lead us to change. Through the endurance it takes to truly change, we the newly teachable can learn to see our children's shortcomings not as offenses against us personally but as cries for mercy — a mercy we are equipped to share through the very practice of those Beatitudes. Through repentance, we don't just intellectually understand why we should be gentle. We now have real-life experience with the rupture/repair cycle so vital to having the types of real relationships with our children that we have not yet had the opportunity to have with our parents.

So what about those relationships with our parents? Where does mercy come in there? Because child abuse is the result of personal sin, personal holiness — attained through repentance and lived out through mercy — is the antidote. Holiness is the antidote to the wounds we received, the wounds we have inflicted on our own children out of our own woundedness, and the inoculation against further disconnectedness from our sons and daughters. Maybe our parents will see us pursuing holiness through repentance and mercy, rupture and repair, and desire that good for themselves.

But how will we know if they do?

Louder Than Words
Each time you read about mercy being available only to those who fear the Lord enough to repent, you may have heard a sin-

ful parent yelling in the shadows of your memory something along the lines of, "I said I'm sorry! What more do you want from me?" Your desire to love your neighbor and show mercy is likely at war with your sense of justice. To confuse matters more, you may have a parent or two in your life who, when confronted with how they've hurt you, demand that you forgive them right then, right now. They may even know enough of the Bible to come at you with Luke 17:4, in which Jesus says, "And if [your brother] wrongs you seven times in one day and returns to you seven times saying, 'I am sorry,' you should forgive him."

There is tension in the life of the survivor of family abuse and dysfunction, the tension between filial loyalty and the way things are "supposed to be" in families, versus the God-given duty to protect one's own children, which sometimes means protecting oneself in order to stay holy enough to be a connected parent. A selfish parent often will say to an adult child who sets up boundaries that those boundaries are selfish, unloving, and not Christlike. So let's take a look at what is Christlike in a relationship between an adult striving to live the Beatitudes for her own sake and the sake of her children while trying to manage boundaries around an unrepentant sinner like an abusive parent. First of all, if it's not yet clear, allow me to reassure you that God offers mercy to the repentant, but only to the *truly repentant*. How can we tell what's true repentance? True repentance can't be faked, reveals itself in word and action, and humbly accepts consequences for past sins.

We can't fake repentance

In Hosea 6:6, God tells us, "For it is loyalty that I desire, not sacrifice, / and knowledge of God rather than burnt offerings." God didn't like receiving burnt offerings from people who would then turn around and offer their next animal sacrifice to some false god. God wants genuine relationship with us, not lip service. He knows we can never outdo him in generosity, but he also wants us to get to know him and care about him (see 1 Pt 5:7 for more on God's actual care for you).

When we cast aside our denials and let ourselves see how much God hurts not just on our behalf but also is hurt by us, our hearts may at last be softened to accept his love for us beyond commandments and into Beatitude. True repentance provides a pudding full of proof. Our children will see this when we initiate the rupture/repair cycle with them. God has given us authority to teach them, and so we must teach them this vital aspect of healthy relationships. We must do so lovingly, modeling repentance and following through with merciful understanding rather than un-meek domineering. We do not, however, have authority to teach our parents. The Fourth Commandment only goes one way, and that authority to command obedience expires once both parents and children are adults. Calling back to meekness and boundaries, there is nothing you can do to change your parents if they do not choose to participate in the rupture/repair cycle with you. Begging them to be godly and treat you differently or raging at them for their failures is, in fact, a violation of meekness. Mercy doesn't overlook sin. Mercy sees sin honestly and steps away from it.

True repentance is clearly visible in word and action

Yes, Jesus said in Luke 17 that we must accept the apology of the brother who sins against us seven times, but we need to look honestly at what is meant by the word "apology." If I tell my child, "I love you" with my lips but then deliberately leave her unfed, unclothed, and unsheltered by the warmth of my arms, that love is clearly a lie. This kind of neglectful parent often defends herself later, saying, "I did my best!" Even if that was that parent's "best," obviously that best wasn't love. The Bible is full of examples, of contrasts between people who offered lip service to God versus those who humbly gave him their hearts: Esau versus Jacob, Israel's sons versus Joseph, Saul versus David (and Saul versus Jonathan, if you're looking for a biblical example of a child breaking the cycle of family dysfunction), the whole nation of Israel versus the prophets. Jesus stayed in Zacchaeus's house, hung out with the Samaritan woman at the well, and let the sinful woman anoint his feet because they all *repented*. He let the rich young man, however, go back to his possessions. The Pharisees he called vipers (see Mt 23:33), unseen graves (Mt 23:27), blind guides (Mt 23:16), and fools (Mt 23:17). He let Judas betray him and then, rather than repent, take his own life. Jesus gave them all plenty of chances to repent. They all refused. Jesus, meekest of the meek, kindest of the kind, gentlest of the gentle, accepted their refusal.

Our next task in this Beatitude, then, is to once again check our own lives first, then with loving authority at our own children's choices, and then with value for our and our children's safety, we are permitted to consider the effects of our own parents' sins. Through our own repentance, are we showing our children the truth that they're being parented by fellow sinners? Do we keep our consciences sensitive by apologizing when we ought and making amends quickly and clearly, especially with our children? When our children do sin, are we disciplining with meekness rather than control, including never allowing them to experience their emotions? It's also worth pointing out that a child's flaws often bother us because, through them, God is trying to teach us something about ourselves. Are we listening for those lessons? Are we modeling teachability as well as sensitivity of conscience so that the rupture/repair cycle can draw us closer to one another and the God who wants us all holy?

Regarding our relationship with our parents, are their behaviors consistent with the Beatitudes? Are they learning holiness or resisting it? Are they allowing us to have our emotions rather than trying to overpower them out of us? Are they actively seeking to discover right from wrong and choose the former, especially in their relationships with us and our children? If yes, thank God that you can engage in the rupture/repair cycle with them. If not, however, remember how Jesus accepted the refusals of the Pharisees, the rich young man, and Judas. If the all-merciful Christ let those people leave him, you can respond with the same meekness. In fact, you must.

The truly repentant humbly accepts consequences for past sins

David willingly suffered the loss of his son as a consequence for how he abused Bathsheba and murdered Uriah. The Prodigal Son begged his father *not* to restore him to sonship but just to hire him on as a worker. Peter, after denying Jesus three times, accepted his eventual martyrdom, in fact seeking to make his own crucifixion even more painful than Christ's by asking to be crucified upside-down. All of these people (or characters, in the case of the Prodigal) demonstrate how humans can adopt Jesus' approach to relationship with him, because these people "did not regard equality with God something to be grasped" (Phil 2:6). The truly repentant person does not expect any right to erase any consequence for their sins. By their humility, acceptance of others' emotional reality and boundaries, and honest admission of the truth of the injustice that has sprung from their actions, the truly repentant honor God's place as Creator and Lord of us all. They seek his justice. They crave it.

Once again, practicing all the other Beatitudes thus far will make way in your heart for you to accept the consequences of your sins. All you need is a heart to learn God's ways, a heart for Christ's movement in your own emotional life and the emotional lives of any people you've hurt, an acknowledgment of the boundaries that you've violated in your failures against meekness, and a conscience sensitive enough to discern when it's time to apologize. A heart so shaped will even seek consequences in the form of making proper amends, should those consequences not immediately present themselves. Imagine being a child parented by this level of humility! Simply by living this way with your own children, you give them an example to live up to, an example of healthy holiness humble enough to build honest relationships through rupture/repair. Should our children, fellow sinners that they are, make choices not to follow such example, we do have authority to correct them; but blessedly, Jesus has shown us how to make those corrections in confident, compassionate love — mercy — rather than through tyranny.

How can you know if the parent who offers apologies is truly repentant? Because that parent will not demand or even expect mercy from you. The truly repentant would never demand mercy because they fully accept that they don't deserve it. It is not unreasonable, and certainly not unmerciful, to limit or even cut off contact with an unrepentant abusive parent. If the parent in question remains unrepentant, Jesus is asking you to be the gardener of the fig tree, giving that parent a chance to remember the finite window that is theirs in which to repent. Indeed, the same parent may repent one day, but if that repentance is real, that parent would never presume a right of entry back into your life and the life of his or her grandchildren. A parent who rails against whatever boundaries you put in place is only proving to you his lack of true repentance.

We ought not grasp at equality with God. God deeply desires our repentance so that he can do his favorite thing ever: Pour mercy on sin. Because God made us in his image, he also made us to share that same mercy with others, which means that when we recognize parents, children, or our own sinful selves are approaching with true repentance, we get to enjoy that same rupture/repair cycle God loves so much. We get to be the ones pouring out mercy. However, God is meek. He respects the choices we make. If God will not force mercy on the unrepentant abuser, neither should we. This is why he teaches us to look for those signs of repentance in our relationships and ourselves. When we see sincerity, clarity, and humility, we can know with confidence when to pour out his mercy, that "I forgive you. I know it's hard to be this human." We know that rupture/repair has begun.

We also will know, just as Jesus did, when to let those we love walk away.

So Now What?

In this Beatitude, Jesus promises mercy for the merciful. As we can see, though, mercy is a gift given only to the repentant. How can we become merciful — become full of mercy — if the people in our lives who sin the most have positioned themselves not to receive the mercy they so desperately need? We can only become filled with mercy by becoming well-practiced in repentance ourselves. We break the cycle of dysfunction, which is just a cycle of pride, denial, poor boundaries, and injustice, by finding those sinful things in our own choices, owning them, seeking forgiveness from God and man, and then making amends without constraint. We repent, and we are filled with mercy. We also give our children the gift of a good example as well as freedom from the false guilt our parents unjustly pushed off on to us.

In fact, their destructive example may have left us with thoughts that we need to reorient in the light of God's mercy. We have been so poisoned by the bad boundaries of abusive parents that we may have inherited their lopsided definition of what guilt even is. We have been taught that guilt is the feeling that tells us to lie when the truth makes others uncomfortable. The reality is that guilt is the feeling that tells us after we've sinned that we need to repent. If we have trouble seeing our own sins because all we seem to see are the sins of others against us, then we must beg God for help so that we can repent and receive mercy. I like to call this "praying for a holy guilt." A holy guilt opens our eyes to the disaster our choices have made of our lives. A holy guilt draws us closer to Christ, not further away.

A holy guilt is our first step into rupture/repair. It frees us to understand the depths of our own sinfulness so that we can repent, but it also will not excuse those who have sinned against us.

What are some positive choices we can make so that we may remain filled with God's mercy but not deny the reality created by the actions of the unrepentant?

We forgive, in the sense that we leave the vengeance to God. We let go of our ideas of revenge on our parents. We refrain from passive-aggressive comments. We don't try to use our rage to change them. It won't work anyway. It will only make them feel justified in their poor treatment of us.

We acknowledge that we are free to rebuke our parents when they sin against us, but we accept that they are free to remain unrepentant.

We pray that our abusers experience holy guilt so that they can repent. This means that we ask God to show them mercy by opening their eyes to the reality of their sin.

We thank God for showing us our own sins, thus healing and protecting us from moral injury and further sins against others, especially our own children.

We curb the wish to see others "burn in hell," and instead pray that they will be purified enough to enter heaven. When people ask if I've forgive my mother for her abuse, I reply with what I've told God over the years, that "I want to see her in heaven — but not a minute before."

In godly mercy, we are free to explore the wisdom and value of going "low contact" or "no contact" with adult family members who regularly treat us unjustly. If those family members remain unrepentant, they choose to forgo God's mercy. To show them this reality might be just the mercy you've been praying for, that they will finally understand the cost of their sins. If you get so flustered around them that you have extraordinary difficulty remaining virtuous, consider going no contact with them in order to protect your own soul from sin. You also have the option to reduce contact with them so that you remain available to them but make your expectations of your relationship with them more realistic.

In our relationships with our own children, we must pray for the experience of a holy guilt, so that we can repent of the ways we unjustly cried out our pain against other innocents, especially spouses and children.

We must model healthy, unconditional apologies to our children, so that they can see that we take our choices as seriously as God does. See the signs of your own sin against your family, especially your children. Apologize and start making reparation now, before they tell you that you need to ... and before they go and write a book about you.

When you lock your heart into the freedom that comes from repentance, the skies clear. You can see the difference God has made between mercy and appeasement. Only one of those saves us from our worst selves, and it's not appeasement.

Facing That Sword

My father ran away from repairing his relationship with me because he was too afraid of the guilt involved in admitting that he loved his house, an object, more than he loved his daughter, a priceless gift God had entrusted to his responsibility. So he denied his failings to me, but most of all to himself. This is not a rare occurrence. So many of us balk at the idea that we have hurt others deeply. So rather than face down that reality, face down the flaming sword standing between our troubled consciences and peace, we convince ourselves that there is no sin. And yet those who do this never find peace or joy. They only find more sins to deny. They never face that sword. It's like David says in Psalm 36:

> Sin directs the heart of the wicked man;
>   his eyes are closed to the fear of God.
> For he lives with the delusion:
>   his guilt will not be known and hated.

Empty and false are the words of his mouth;
he has ceased to be wise and do good. (vv. 2–4)

Harmful parenting is a result not of culture or a past of being abused but of personal sin. Jesus is truth. Those who deny the truth about their sin and refuse to repent simply cannot be a part of his body. It's just not possible. It's not part of God's personality to graft in a person who isn't sincerely seeking connection with him. Remember our chapter on the meek inheriting the earth? Jesus is the one who is truly meek. He has boundaries and keeps them. He lets other people make their choices, even if those choices disconnect them from him. Mercy is only available to those who fear God enough to repent, to change their ways and strive to amend the bad they've done. It's worth repeating: God's love is unconditional. His mercy is not.

We can, however, rest in the knowledge that God is judge. Yes, he gives us signs to help us identify repentance in the actions of those around us. However, in the end, God will judge all hearts, even those that seem hardened until their very last beats. God does indeed make all things new. He does so in ways we don't expect, sometimes through deathbed conversions, sometimes through letting relationships crumble so that a sinner can at last see, in his solitude, the reality of his own wounds rather than being distracted by the sins of others.

Sometimes God changes hearts and restores relationships here on earth. Sometimes he asks us to let go of relationships that should have been healing, comforting, and nurturing but, through the stiff-necked choices of unrepentant sinners, simply aren't. Showing the reality of mercy to those who habitually betray God's love for us purges our hearts of unhealthy attachment to what should have been, and frees us to accept the post-traumatic resurrection that God has built out of our pain. This makes room for the joy that is mercy, both in our own hearts and between us and our children. This is the beginning of purity of heart, and that is the Beatitude we will study next.

HOLY FAMILY MOMENT
The Finding in the Temple (Lk 2:41–52)

Now here's a recipe for how to recover from a dangerous family understanding. A tween boy goes missing, probably due to parental miscommunication, and when he's found, he explains his absence with what might be taken as some pretty sassy backtalk. *I'll* show *you* your father's house!

Okay, that's the knee-jerk response I'd be inclined to give in such a situation because I'm still training my brain to find the good in what my kids do, even their mistakes and sins. Joseph and Mary, however, had healthy habits of trust in God's providence, especially when it concerned the child entrusted to their care. Mary didn't accuse or punish. She simply and honestly opened up to Jesus about her feelings. He responded with his own questions. They responded, again simply and honestly, that they didn't understand. He responded with trust in and obedience to them. Simple, honest sharing on all sides is the key to healing mercy in all relationships, especially in the family.

BEATITUDE BASIC WORKSHOP
Repentance

1. Journal in hand, pray the Prayer for the Gift of Holy Guilt (this section's prayer). Ask God to open your eyes to the difference between guilt and shame. Write down what you discover.
2. Journal about a flaw you see in your child. Spend some time in written prayer, asking God to show you what you can learn about your own sins through

how this flaw evokes your emotions. Continue to examine your own life for that sin and others first before correcting your child.

3. While Jesus does indeed want us all to be one, he wants us to be one in truth, not in false comfort. Just as you can repent of sins that endanger your soul, you can repent of relationships for the same reason. Seek wise counsel and consider prayerfully whether or not your relationships with unrepentant parents are a threat to your heart, your parents' souls, or your children's well-being.

PRAYER FOR THE GIFT OF HOLY GUILT

My Lord and my God,
Fill me with a holy guilt.
I am filled with shame of my own making,
A shame that only speaks of me
And turns me away from your generous love.
Fill me so full with a holy guilt
That comes from you alone,
That serves as both map and compass,
That there is no more room for shame or lies or poor self-comfort.

Fill me with holy guilt,
With your good Word,
So that I may follow you as closely as this exile allows
And when I breathe my last,
I find myself purified of self and resting in your eternal embrace.

SAINT-SPIRATION
Blessed Laura Vicuña

How many of us have disclosed the types of abuse we have experienced, only to hear our listeners respond with something like, "The person who did that to you should go to hell"? The joyful life does not take that approach, even toward the souls of child abusers. How could this be possible? One teenager, betrayed by her own mother, shows us how. Blessed Laura Vicuña is often called "the other Maria Goretti," but that leaves out the part of her story that makes her a model of mercy for victims, specifically victims of family abuse.

After Laura's father's death, Laura's pregnant, widowed mother fled war-torn Chile. She sought safety in Argentina for herself and her two children, including Laura's unborn sister, and took a job in the household of a wealthy man named Mora, who soon offered Laura's mother, Mercedes, protection in exchange for becoming his mistress. Rather than hold out for God's providence, Mercedes accepted. Soon, however, Mercedes was not enough to satisfy this man, and he began to pursue eleven-year-old Laura. Laura fended him off, but at one point, even her mother asked her to give in to him. As she resisted Mora's lust and suffered betrayal from her own mother, she asked her confessor at her boarding school for permission to offer her life to God for her mother's salvation. With that permission granted, Laura soon became so ill that she was sent away from her boarding school and back to her mother — and Mora. A sick Laura died after being beaten to death for daring to run away from him. That very night, her mother saw the depths of what she had done. She ran to confession and turned her life around from that point on.

The unique mercy an abuse survivor can give changes souls. It can change the world, if we put our pain to work.[38]

---

38. Brian O'Neel, "Blessed Laura Vicuña," *39 New Saints You Should Know* (Cincinnati: Servant, 2010), 26–28.

– 8 –
BLESSED ARE THE CLEAN OF HEART

For They Will See God

Beatitude Basic: Gratitude

> Unless the LORD build the house,
> they labor in vain who build.
> Unless the LORD guard the city,
> in vain does the guard keep watch.
> — Psalm 127:1

Time After Time

My first job that wasn't babysitting was working in nutritional services of the nursing home up the street from my house. I hated that job. Hated it. My fellow dietary aides were all levels of cruel to me, up to and including sexual harassment. But I was stuck with that job, my parents decreed, until I could get my driver's license and drive myself to something better. Needless to say, while I was never officially late, I certainly dragged my feet to my shifts.

I don't know what possessed my parents to do this, but one day, as I got out of the shower to get dressed and leave for work, they shared a rare moment of alliance. I opened the bathroom door and immediately heard them both shouting to me over the drone of whatever TV show they were watching, "You're late! You're late! You're going to get written up! Hurry!"

They told me the time. Less than ten minutes until the start of my shift? I gasped and ran to my room to rush the rest of my preparations. I'd have to skip makeup. Forget the curling iron. What little time I had could only be spent dressing. I'd have to jam the back of my hair into its hairnet on the run up the street. While I was madly digging around for the maroon bow tie that was part of my uniform, I finally looked at my clock — the clock I regularly set fifteen minutes fast so that I could avoid incurring my father's wrath for any sins against punctuality. According to my clock, after doing the appropriate arithmetic, I still had the better part of half an hour until my shift started. It took ten minutes to walk from my front door to the time clock.

I ran out to look at the kitchen clock, the one I had assumed my parents had been reading. I returned to the living room and asked, "Why did you tell me it was later than this?"

"We just didn't want you to be late," my mother explained.

I left for work, still not understanding why my parents would have outright lied to me about something so unnecessary. All I knew was that, on that walk up the hill to the nursing home, I vowed that I would never lie to my own children, if I had them. As a parent now, I understand why they made that decision to deceive me and to deceive themselves into thinking that they were doing the right thing: preventing my foot-dragging from getting me in trouble at work. God in his generosity has also seen fit to help me understand why their motives were false. They pointed toward a false goal.

God longs to make all things new in our families. For our part, we must choose by his grace to aim toward the one true goal — God himself.

The Truth about Purity

Part of having been formed in a dysfunctional family involves having a dictionary of bad definitions locked inside of our minds. God wants to open those doors and let in the light. God also wants us to see his face, and so in this Beatitude he promises us that privilege if we will pursue cleanliness of heart. First, for brevity's sake, let's compress the idea of cleanliness of heart into the word "purity," which is a word with its own baggage in our current culture, but hopefully we can unpack that enough here to make it manageable and even attractive to the soul pursuing God after a childhood spent enduring abuse and other falsehoods. In order to get our heads around what it means to be pure, let's first unpack three things that purity *isn't.*

Purity doesn't mean being anyone's idea of perfect.

Maybe you were mocked for having bad skin, an eating disorder, too much hair, too little hair, or for being bad at sports. Maybe you were given a purity ring sometime in high school and, before you even understood the meaning of the word chastity, were pressured to promise that you would never have sex outside of marriage — and then you didn't keep that promise. Maybe you were harshly disciplined for something that may have been legitimate sin, but the discipline came from a place of control rather than a place of guiding you toward heaven while still respecting your boundaries. None of this is a facet of God's personality. If you're having trouble accepting this reality, go back and read the chapter on all the blessings in store for the meek. Part of being meek is understanding that this present world is fallen and imperfect.

Being pure also doesn't mean you've never been sinned against

It doesn't matter if you have been beaten with a belt, raped, verbally humiliated, or suffered countless other indignities. That does not affect *your* purity. Jesus himself affirms for us, "It is not what enters one's mouth that defiles that person; but what comes out of the mouth is what defiles one. ... But the things that come out of the mouth come from the heart, and they defile. For from the heart come evil thoughts, murder, adultery, unchastity, theft, false witness, blasphemy" (Mt 15:11, 18–19). What others do *to* you does not affect who you are in Christ. *Your* choices impact that relationship with him, but others' choices can't.

Lastly, purity isn't an excuse for a lack of self-control

I remember when, during my days as a young parish youth minister, a certain pop musician performed on national television. She opened her performance by telling the audience that she wanted to perform songs "from a very pure place." This performer then proceeded to sing her angry song for the television audience, a song full of explicit lyrics, highlighted by a certain word that rhymes with "fire truck." The following morning, the sixty-something parish secretary cornered my twenty-something self and demanded to know what this singer meant by calling her work "pure." At that moment, I was struck with the reality that the previous generation's definition of the word "pure" did not mean the same thing that "pure" meant to my generation. I tried to explain that, to Generation X, "pure" meant brutally honest, unadulterated emotion. To us, "pure" did not refer to any sort of moral purity.

Depending on the culture in which you were raised, either the larger, national or regional culture or the culture specific to your family, you may have received the idea that purity is just letting it all hang out, doing what you want and consequences be damned. Reality, alas, is that consequences can be damning if we refuse to cultivate self-control. Just because we tell ourselves that our words and actions won't affect anyone doesn't mean that they won't.

Knowing what purity *isn't* does play a vital role in the life of one pursuing God's face, not only in recognizing the stamp of his image in your humanity but also in building a deeply connected relationship with him. However, recognizing what something *isn't* does not immediately translate to recognizing the nature of a thing. This is true for the nature of purity. We know that the pursuit of purity does matter. God tells us so. Revelation 21:27 describes heaven as a place that nothing unclean can enter. So what does it mean to be pure? Specifically, what does it mean for the survivor of family abuse and dysfunction to pursue purity of heart?

Stay on Target

Purity of heart means you only have one goal: heaven.

Seriously. It's just that simple. You want heaven for yourself. You also want heaven for others. You want heaven for all, no matter how difficult it is. It's the pearl of great price for which you will sell anything, because in comparison, everything else is worthless. More importantly, heaven is your goal because you want to be united with the good and eternal God, not simply because you fear hell or want eternal comfort. We survivors of family abuse may find that last bit a sticky wicket. I know I did and often still do. This is because I was not parented with purity of intention. I was not parented with heaven in mind. As a result, I was not parented in a way that promoted loving attachment in healthy relationships because the people teaching (and largely failing) me in the school of love weren't themselves aiming for connection with the truth. They only wanted immediate control, which is not how God made us to live — or love.

We shouldn't be surprised that others' sins make it hard for us to see God's goodness. Remember that leper whom Jesus healed and then asked him to keep the healing private, and the healed man promptly spread the word so far and wide about this healer that other people who needed to see Jesus had to journey into the desert to do so? The leper's skin was healed, but his heart? Not quite. He was not strong enough, did not yet have a pure enough heart, to say no to his own impulses. Jesus worked around that, of course, but consequences remained for the people not yet healed.

Purity strengthens like nothing else can. We even say that something pure *is* strong: pure alcohol or pure essential oil, for example. We also see why the pursuit of purity can be difficult for those of us from backgrounds that didn't teach secure love. Like the leper, we can't imagine our maladaptive survival techniques would do any harm, and surely we know better! That nice healer guy doesn't know what he's asking! Our view of purity spins off of that mindset: Why would we be able to imagine wanting to spend eternity with a God who put us with people who failed to show us pure love? The door to the purity waiting to bloom inside our hearts remains locked.

The key to unlocking this door is gratitude. Purity of heart is wanting heaven. Wanting heaven means wanting God's perfect will. Wanting God's perfect will means that we surrender the idea that we know everything, and we give up our entitlement to having things our way. Giving up our own way means seeing the good in all the things, even and especially the difficult things, that God chooses for us. Seeing the good in all things makes us grateful for everything that happens to us. It makes us grateful for everything that *has* happened to us. With a pure heart, we can freely say the words of Israel's son Joseph, "Even though you meant harm to me, God meant it for good, to achieve this present end, the survival of many people" (Gn 50:20).

By purifying our motives, thoughts, and intentions, we turn

our eyes away from our own self-centeredness and onto the face of God. Hence Jesus attaches the blessing of seeing God's face directly to his blessing on the clean of heart. See? Jesus knows what he's doing, especially when it comes to redeeming a fallen world. Smart guy. Purity transforms our pain to gratitude. Gratitude transforms our relationships, in both our families of origin and our families of destination. Such transformation is vital to the survivor who wants to be the stopping point on the timeline of generational abuse. That transformation takes time and practice, though. Thankfully Jesus put poverty of spirit and teachability at the top of his Beatitudes list.

What's My Motivation?

We are so blessed that our parish has a perpetual adoration chapel. I'd dropped by over the years here and there, after dropping my kids off at their parish religious education classes or just while running errands in the neighborhood. With homeschooling three young children and still trying to do my writing work, I'd always figured I was too busy to manage a whole hour a week, plus the hour of round-trip commute time since we live out in the country, to fit regular adoration of the Blessed Sacrament into my life. I'd been truly struggling with my writing and my homeschooling, however, when a plea came out to fill in several hours when the chapel had been sitting empty. I looked at the holes in the schedule, talked it over with my husband, and I decided I'd take one hour per week, adoring Jesus in the chapel. After all, people had promised me, "You can't outdo God in generosity. Give him one hour, and you'll get back so much more!"

I believed them, but I believed them *my* way, not God's. I told myself that if I gave Jesus this extra time in addition to the prayer routine I already had in place, surely he would give me the time I seemed to lack to make my homeschooling and writing schedules work out with any peace. Imagine my surprise when my schedule didn't actually feel any looser. In those first six months or so, I was shocked — shocked, I tell you! — to discover that those two extra hours a week (remember the commute time) didn't translate to, say, five additional hours of time magically appearing in my schedule so that I could get more done.

I laugh at myself now, thinking of how I wondered what kind of game God was playing here, roping me in to giving away two hours of my already tight schedule just to sit with him for only one of those hours. When was he going to pay up on his side of the deal anyway? At last, one dim morning in the adoration chapel, I asked him point-blank what he was doing with this time I was giving him. Was I ever going to get any of it back? The answer I received was to think of my husband and children and how much it hurts me when they reject spending time with me because they, fallen humans that they are, feel like they have better things to do than cultivate our relationships, or they only spend time with me when I'm doing something that enables their laziness and self-focus.

Ouch. Well, that was convicting.

I tell you this story to bring home a point. We fallen humans tend to see our relationship with God as transactional. He gives us something, so we give back. In return, if we give him something, he owes us, right? We want God to give us what will make us feel better, and we want that better feeling now. Anything less is contemptible. If someone gets more than I do, I get angry. If someone gets worse than I do, I am relieved that I escaped a similar doom that time. Alas, this isn't relating to God. This is using God. This way of relating to God is the very definition of impurity.

That said, I have since experienced that, when I turn even my transactional demands to a loving God, he redeems them. I went to the adoration chapel greedy, but I came out transformed. He turned my greed to gratitude. I mean, eventually. God took my greed for time, success, and recognition and purified it, opening yet another door deeper into his love for me. We often think that if we do bad things from a good motive, that God will bless it anyway. That may be true sometimes, but the reverse can be true as well: If we do good things from an impure motive, God will transform that motive and thus our hearts, into something pure. He will clean us up. Being made in his image and likeness, we sure do clean up good.

We survivors of family abuse and dysfunction were raised to believe that love was conditional at best. The only way to get something pleasant was to be good enough — or to be clever enough to avoid the bad. We get what we get because *we* got it. Alas, this transactionality is destructive to the human heart because God did not make us for transactions; he made us for relationship. When we make choices from a place of getting what we deserve, we are likely to see our good things as ours, not as gifts freely given by a generous God. We also are likely to see our difficulties as punishments for not being good enough. God does not love us that way. God loves us in a way we can't earn or lose. When we make relationship with him, rather than immediate comfort, our goal we default to a state of gratitude.

God's love is pure. God also challenges us to love our neighbors like he does, and our families are our closest neighbors. He asks us to love them as we are invited to love him, with purity of intention, not because we should have to earn their love, and certainly not because they should earn ours. When we love tantrum-prone toddlers, tantrum-prone teenagers, and tantrum-prone adults with purity, we are set free. We stop expecting to get anything out of them because all we want is the chance to spend heaven with the gifts that they are to us, even in their difficult behaviors — even when they remind us how difficult our behaviors are. Now, if you think that last sentence just negated my last chapter, where I showed that mercy is only for the repentant, and thus we need not maintain active relationships with our unrepentant parents, read on, fellow survivor. Read on.

Three for the Price of One
Jesus put blessings for the pure-hearted after blessings for the merciful for a very solid reason. When we strive to be merciful as our Father is merciful, God opens our eyes to the reality of sin because there is no mercy without repentance. Like I used to tell the second-graders I was preparing for first reconciliation, "If nothing is your fault, and you never do anything wrong, and anything you *do* do wrong is someone else's fault, then you aren't ready for first reconciliation. That means you're not ready for first Eucharist. You have to have some sins first." What's true for second-graders is true for us all. You're not ready for mercy until you repent of your sin.

Once our eyes are opened to sin, we may become so uncomfortable with the reality of our own sins that we decide it would be a whole lot easier to focus on others' problems instead of our own. Seeing others' sins without repenting of our own is not wanting heaven. When we reorient our intentions from making ourselves feel better at any cost to gaining heaven at any cost, we not only connect with our own need of mercy, but that mercy comes in and purifies us so that we can see the truth — which is just another word for the face of God.

In other words, by working on purity within ourselves, we automatically contribute to the purity of the people around us, the people God tasks us with loving in his name. Teachability opens us to identifying disordered thought patterns and submitting them to God's truth. Emotional connection helps us accept that truth. Meekness tells us we can't use our emotions to change others. Mercy tells us we don't have to. Purity tells us we can still love them even if they don't change, but purity also protects us from ever again enabling their sins. This is because purity orients the heart to pleasing God, not pleasing others if their wants aren't rightly ordered toward heaven. Purity makes us grateful for our heartbreaks just as much as our joys.

How does purity, then, help us parent our children out of the cycle of generational abuse? The obvious answer is that we provide our children with a good example, but purity goes beyond even that. Purity of heart also helps us become purely ourselves with our children and not just some reaction against what was done to us when we were in their helpless shoes. If we never let our kids see us angry because we don't want to become our own angry parents, then we never model how to express anger appropriately. Purity provides us with what to do in any given situation rather than leaving us to flail inwardly against what not to do.

Wanting heaven for our children also puts into perspective the type of support we ought to give them as they proceed through all their stages of development. We now see even our kids' worst moods and most destructive behaviors as gifts, as opportunities to build relationship through rupture/repair. Because we no longer need to have things our way all the time, we lose the desire to control our children in an overbearing way and instead are free to love them with gratitude for the gifts they are. This in turn makes it easier to let go of them in their own decisions as they mature. Best of all, purity of heart makes us better role models, more worthy of trust, because the sincerity of our interest in their good will prove itself unselfish and for their own sake. We will more readily welcome the fact that they're not really our children in the first place but beloved children of the most high God.

Purity of heart has great power to transform our relationships with our families of origin as well. Once we want heaven for everyone, even those who committed grave abuses against us, purity can turn sadness and anger into gratitude. When that transformation needs to take a long time because the hurt is so deep, purity of intention reminds us that God's will is our good, and even the lingering pain that comes from the slow healing of deep wounds has its purpose. Eventually, the practice of purity frees us to forgive deep hurts, leading us into the deepest layers of mercy for our sinful parents and for our own sins — often enough *through* our own sins.

When we want heaven for our parents, we start seeking to please God rather than appease them. We no longer excuse or enable their cruelty, manipulation, and immaturity. Sometimes, as discussed in previous chapters, pointing our parents toward heaven means limiting their access to our hearts and our children. Purity strengthens our resolve in such painful cases. Purity keeps our eyes on the face of our heavenly Father who will never fail us. Best of all, when we fix our eyes on heaven, we can cultivate gratitude for what good our parents have given us, even if the only discernible good was the gift of a life to spend in the redeeming, unconditionally loving arms of the crucified and risen Christ.

When we seek to honor God in all that we do, we don't just open ourselves up to the heavenly embrace. We shine a light for the generations that sandwich ours. As the middle of that sandwich, we are held in tension between our children — immature, still-growing, fallen humans — on one side, and our parents — disordered, stiff-necked, fallen humans — on the other. Both sides will send us requests that may trigger our defenses and tempt us away from seeking God's face.

In a clean heart, temptation to surrender to others' disordered demands loses much of its power. A pure heart remembers that the sinners around us are gifts chosen for us by a loving God, and once we learn whatever God is trying to teach us through this gift, we can be grateful rather than resentful. When we resist others' sins against us, those trying to hurt us don't get that false comfort that they were expecting. There is a chance that such negative reinforcement may make those people reconsider sinning against us next time. We will be free to face false accusations of "selfishness" when we resist the selfishness of others, because we will have the confidence to examine our motives and know they are holy — or if they aren't, to turn back to the earlier Beatitudes and reorient until our hearts are purified.

Pure and Simple
A pure heart is distracted by nothing and grateful for everything. A pure heart pursues goodness and truth at all costs because even pain is a gift. Once God has led us to confidence in the goodness of our drives and desires, we are free to be transparent to others. We have nothing to hide because we see God's face. We know truth, and it is making us free at every moment we keep our eyes fixed on it. What we think and what we do are largely in accord with one another. In this newfound freedom, we will make more choices with an eye toward honoring God as a generous giver of gifts. Unfortunately, this translates to angering people whose motives are not so ordered. God tells us to love our enemies, but he never said they would stop discrediting us just because we now love them in truth rather than in appeasement.

A heart must be clean in order to be ready for the next Beatitude Jesus gives us because a clean heart is a grateful heart, a secure heart, a confident heart. The immature behaviors our children may throw our way will not disturb us quite the way they used to because we know our job is to point our kids to heaven, not just to escape any discomfort their behaviors might cause. The hurts that unappeased parents may send our way can no longer touch us because we know they are unfounded. A clean heart is a heart at peace, which makes peace in the lives of all we meet — even in the hearts of those we've had to release.

HOLY FAMILY MOMENT
Mary Meets Jesus on the Way to the Crucifixion
Tradition tells us that Mary met Jesus as he was paraded through town to his place of execution, and common sense tells us that this must be true. Of course, the perfect mother would stand by her son

when he was in agony. The two purest hearts ever made to beat of human flesh meet under the worst circumstances ever endured by a human family. She did not deserve to see her son suffer this way. He did not deserve to see his undeserved pain reflected in his mother's eyes. And yet neither fought, protested or belittled those who had brought them to this way of sorrow because he knew and she trusted. There could be no earthly happiness or comfort that could ever outweigh God's will for either of them, no matter how painful the execution of that will could be.

Purity of heart puts all things in the right order. It tells us that the pain God has chosen for us has its place in his plan. It tells us that our pain matters and will make a glorious, joyful difference, not just for ourselves but for those at whose hands we suffer. We just have to hold on to him and keep our eyes fixed on the face of Jesus, who also knows undeserved suffering and the ultimate pain of sin.

BEATITUDE BASIC WORKSHOP
Gratitude

1. Journal about any areas where you need to examine your idea of what it means to be pure. Do you ever feel unworthy because of your imperfections, whether in mind, body or spirit? Do you ever find yourself being cruel but excusing yourself for it under the guise of "honesty"? Ask God to heal you.

2. Develop a practice of making sure your conscience is formed not toward earthly appeasement of others but toward inviting everyone you meet, including the person in the mirror, to eternal joy in heaven. You can do this by studying Scripture, the *Catechism*, and seeking counsel from trusted friends who seem to have eternal priorities rather than temporal ones.

3. Journal about relational interactions that trouble you,

especially with your children and parents. What might God be teaching you about your own motivations through the things that upset you? Are there any desires that are for earthly comfort that you can consider in a different light? What desires for eternal good, or experiences that point us to eternal good, like unconditional love, are aching inside your heart that the people around you are failing to notice? Bring those desires to God in prayer and ask to see how he wants to fulfill and redeem that unresolved pain.

BENEDICTUS – THE CANTICLE OF ZECHARIAH (LK 1:68-79)

Blessed be the Lord, the God of Israel,
　for he has visited and brought redemption to his people.
He has raised up a horn for our salvation
　within the house of David his servant,
even as he promised through the mouth of his holy prophets
　　from of old:
　salvation from our enemies and from the hand of all who
　　hate us,
to show mercy to our fathers
　and to be mindful of his holy covenant
and of the oath he swore to Abraham our father,
　and to grant us that, rescued from the hand of enemies,
without fear we might worship him in holiness and
　righteousness
before him all our days.
And you, child, will be called prophet of the Most High,
　for you will go before the Lord to prepare his ways,
to give his people knowledge of salvation
　through the forgiveness of their sins,

because of the tender mercy of our God
 by which the daybreak from on high will visit us
to shine on those who sit in darkness and death's shadow,
 to guide our feet into the path of peace.

SAINT-SPIRATION: SAINT MARIA GORETTI

The thing that irks me every July 6 is all the people who show up declaring that Saint Maria Goretti was a model of purity because she fought an attacker in order to keep her virginity intact.

Nonsense.

Maria had been pursued by her neighbor Alessandro, who'd been filling his imagination with pornography and then trying to catch Maria alone at every turn. Maria was no weak, helpless thing. This eleven-year-old child threw pots and pans at him to fend him off. When Alessandro finally cornered her, alone, he was armed with a heavy metal file. Maria screamed at him, "No! It is a sin! You will go to hell!"

You will go to hell. Emphasis mine.

Maria knew Jesus well enough to be confident that she was not in eternal danger. She also knew him well enough to be confident that Jesus even wanted this depraved man to go to heaven. While in jail for her murder, Alessandro had a vision of Maria giving him lilies, one for each stab wound he inflicted upon her. At last he confessed his sin, repented, and upon being released from jail, went to Maria's mother to beg her forgiveness. She gave it. After years of penance and humility, he died in peace.

Purity of heart helps us see the value in everyone, even in our enemies — even in ourselves.[39]

---

39. Treasures of the Church, "The Murder," The Pilgrimage of Mercy: Tour of the Major Relics of St. Maria Goretti (website), 2015, mariagoretti.com.

– 9 –
BLESSED ARE THE PEACEMAKERS
For They Will Be Called Children of God

Beatitude Basic: Transparency

Blessed is the man who does not walk
in the counsel of the wicked,
Nor stand in the way of sinners,
nor sit in company with scoffers.
Rather, the law of the LORD is his joy;
and on his law he meditates day and night.
He is like a tree
planted near streams of water,
that yields its fruit in season;
Its leaves never wither;
whatever he does prospers.

— Psalm 1:1–3

The War for Peace

Remember Dawn Eden from our chapter on meekness, the former rock journalist who found healing for her wounds of childhood abuse in the Catholic Faith? In her book *My Peace I Give You*, she talks about how, as her process of conversion was first underway, she found herself becoming, well, an internet troll. She writes about how, in her early blogging days, she lashed out at strangers. "I picked fights with radical feminist bloggers," she writes, "calling them names and attacking them in personal terms." Why did she go after writers on these particular subjects, however? She answers her own question in admitting, "In their praise for what they termed sexual freedom, I saw the elimination of sexual boundaries — the boundaries that, had they been enforced in my childhood home, would have protected me from harm."[40]

In other words, Jesus had shown Dawn the grave injustice in the sexual abuse she had suffered as a child. He also had shown her the injustice served her by her own mother, who had turned a blind eye to the abuse Dawn was suffering right before her very eyes. Dawn's soul was thus awakened to the hunger and thirst for justice named in the fourth Beatitude. Alas, her journey into Jesus' merciful heart had not yet led her to true satisfaction. She lashed out at people who operated from the same mentality of the people who had hurt her both directly and less so, but she was clearly not at peace about it. She instead craved conflict to the point of creating it because she had not yet found the source of satisfaction for that injustice.

As the title of her book suggests, of course, she has since found the font of that satisfaction, life in Christ under the mentorship of the saints. Now she writes from a place of resolving conflict to bring about healing in the lives of her readers and listeners as well as continued healing in her own life. She has since found her

---

40 Eden, *My Peace*, 143.

daughtership in the arms of a loving God who teaches us the value and implementation of healthy boundaries, how to turn from our own sins and work for justice in all our relationships, and how to keep our eyes on the only real goal worth having: ultimate unity with the Creator who loves us into existence. Dawn Eden's life gives us a beautiful example of how the survivor of family abuse and dysfunction can grow not just *in spite of* her wounds but *through* them. By cultivating her love of God, she is being formed in healthy love for neighbor — even for the mother who failed her so badly. This allowed teachability, emotional connection, good boundaries, appreciation for God's power to both limit and save, repentance, and gratitude all to grow in her life. Once all these tools of healthy love grow in the life of even the most wounded among us, peace blooms.

This must be why Jesus places a blessing for peacemakers here in the Beatitudes and no earlier. A life lived in all the previous Beatitudes makes interior peace for the one living them. Once the practice of the first six Beatitudes are in place, the interior peace that follows frees one to face the conflicts that threaten that peace. One who lives the Beatitudes is free to speak truth into denial of all sorts. This aspect of peacemaking is especially important for the family abuse survivor. In order to face the temptations that come in every relationship, but especially those closest to us like our parents and our children, we must have interior peace. To achieve this requires deliberate practice, especially after a childhood of being repeatedly wounded. Thankfully, examples like Eden's and the saints' she talks about in her book (and hopefully the saints I talk about here) offer us survivors abundant hope.

Peace Negotiations

Experiencing and making peace as a survivor is not easy, especially since our relationships and experiences have been so poisoned with sin. Once again, alas, we first must illustrate how certain sinful thought and behavior patterns aren't part of living Beatitude. We should not be surprised, though. As we've seen, especially in the chapter on mercy, the habitual sinner is desperate to convince himself that he has not sinned. This leads the sinner into a strangling labyrinth of denial, specifically denials that choke the truth cried out by the pain of others in a sad attempt to hush the pain screaming inside the morally injured heart of the abuser. From our childhoods all the way up through the present day, any time we may have alluded to our legitimate pain from the choices made by our families of origin, we probably got the same script:

- What is your problem?
- Why can't you just leave that in the past?
- Why are you causing problems?
- Forgive and forget!
- Stop upsetting your mother/father/sister/brother!
- You're the one causing these fights by bringing up all that stuff. Can't you just let bygones be bygones?

We've already examined such responses in the light of Jesus' blessings of mercy on the merciful. That Beatitude does not permit us to ignore sin. Becoming a peacemaker in the face of such denials, however, invites us to look at the abuser's responses to the truth with an eye to what peacemaking isn't. Peace can't be made true when sin is ignored, truth-tellers are silenced, or when self-pity rather than self-donative love rules the relationship. Let's take a deeper look now at what real peacemakers don't do.

Peace Talks
Peacemaking doesn't ignore sin. Sin happens. Acting like it doesn't will never erase its effects. Push them down all you like. Those effects will continue to rise up and confront both the sinner and

the sinned-against. Thus the sinner in denial can never have peace. This is why Admonish the Sinner is one of the seven Spiritual Works of Mercy. To point out another's sin, even if it was decades ago, is to witness to the truth, to provide the sinner with an opportunity to repent and receive mercy. The repentant sinner lives in truth. The repentant sinner, thus, lives in peace.

As parents ourselves, we must keep that before our eyes at all times if we want a truly peaceful relationship with our children. We do well not just to make regular sacramental confession part of our family lives. Regular admittance of our sins against our kids *to* our kids, followed by making sincere reparations for those sins, is perhaps the chief stepping stone on the path to peace in our families. This doesn't just give our children an example of how to be true adults. This also honors the truth of their hurts and reminds them that they are worthy of real love, a love that empties the parent of self and lifts the child up to the perfect heart of God.

However, as children of abusive families, Jesus asks us to make peace by, yes, accepting what blame truly is ours for the fractures in our relationship with our families of origin. Our victimization may explain our sins, but it never excuses it. We receive so much grace when, teachable, we accept the reality of our own sins — hatred, unforgiveness, passive aggression, cruel words — against our parents. That said, Jesus also asks us to make peace by acknowledging the ways we were harmed by our parents' sins. If they remain unrepentant and proceed to tell us that we have nothing to complain about in how they treated us (and, in many cases, still treat us), we can be confident that they are not telling the truth, that they are asking us to live a lie so that they can continue providing themselves with false comfort. False comfort is anything but peace.

In such cases, Jesus also demands that we be vigilant in protecting our children against any sins our parents, in their unrepentant habits, are known to think are their right to commit (see

Mt 18:6). If we ignore our parents' sin in this way, we share in their culpability for their sins against our children — and the harm that our innocent children will then be forced to carry into the generation after theirs. We ignore sin at the peril of all.

The Good Fight

Peacemakers don't press the mute button. I have twin teenage girls. This means there is a certain level of verbal conflict in our house. As they mature, so do their conflicts. Where once they fought over whose turn it is to wash the guinea pigs' water bottles, now they fight over politics and whether or not women should veil before the Blessed Sacrament. Okay, so they also still fight over the guinea pig bottles, but you get the idea. As they mature, and their thoughts become more complex, they have an inborn instinct to hone those thoughts against another's thinking. I used to bark orders at them to stop fighting and make up their minds for them ("*You* clean the bottles! *You* take care of the lettuce! End of discussion!"), but, thank God, I've since seen that, by robbing them of the opportunity to explore healthy conflict, I rob them of their right to build confidence in a safe place: the shelter of a Christ-seeking home. In shutting down their conflicts, I rob them of peacemaking.

A book that really helped me understand the value of healthy conflict in a family was *Building Better Families: A Practical Guide to Raising Amazing Children* by Matthew Kelly of the Dynamic Catholic Institute. First of all, I loved the title because it implies that the children are already amazing and all I have to do is raise them, by which I like to think my job as parent is to raise them up not to some idea of "good kid" but simply raise them to God. Secondly, it hit my heart right in that fear-of-conflict spot when Kelly writes, "Often our approach is peace at any price, which of course is no peace at all.[...] What we need is healthy conflict, and only one thing makes healthy conflict possible: common, unchanging purpose."[41]

The Beatitudes, especially the one before peacemaking — purity of heart — make clear the Christian family's common, unchanging purpose: getting each other to heaven. Holy goals unite us to each other and to the unchanging good that is God. Heaven isn't going anywhere.

However, a family is made up of individuals with free will. Our actions must center on the purpose of getting each other to heaven without leaving ourselves behind — because I am valued by God too. For instance, as a parent, I have a duty to get my children to Mass. This is a holy duty that in and of itself helps a family toward the holy goal of getting each other to heaven. However, beating or belittling the child (or parent) who refuses to go to Mass is a use of one's anger in an effort to obliterate the free will of another. This is an offense against meekness and is decidedly *not* holy. What could a parent do in a case like this? Well, if my children are resisting holiness in some way, I must open the floor for them to tell me why. I must listen and remind them that they are allowed to doubt me because that's how they'll learn to test their own thoughts for the truth. However, sometimes they still have to obey me even if they don't want to, but they are always permitted to try to persuade me, and it is my job to listen to them — not to mute them.

Sometimes they do persuade me. Sometimes they don't. Admittedly, I've only started doing this in recent years, and it's taking what feels like a long time for them to trust that I'm not going to do what I used to do (see above, where I'd decree an end to the conflict, whether the conflict had actually ended or not). They still aren't super inclined to open up to me when they disagree. Parenting is not a sprint but a marathon, so that's okay, and the hurt I feel from their lack of openness is just part of the penance I must experience

41. Matthew Kelly, *Building Better Families: A Practical Guide to Raising Amazing Children* (New York: Beacon Publishing, 2008), 17.

for my sins against them when they were younger. They deserved better than they got from me. I can only resolve to do better. Such a resolution is that holy goal, heaven, that God asks me to share with my family.

This is why, during one particularly heated argument, I interrupted them, not to stop the fight, but to ask the younger twin, "Do you want her to go to heaven?"

Her jaw dropped briefly, but she answered quickly, firmly, "Yes."

I turned to the older one. "Do you want her to go to heaven?"

She paused, too, before answering, "Yes."

I nodded at them. "If you're just trying to get each other to heaven, then fight on."

The nature of their conflicts seems to have changed slightly since then. There's less venom. I can't know their minds — that's the Holy Spirit's job — but I can hope that being reminded that they have a common, holy goal has helped them remember that conflict is good and holy when it serves not the ego but the other's soul. They let each other talk, and they listen a little better.

They still do sometimes try to bully each other into changing their opinions. Hey — they're still teenagers. In children, this is generally developmentally appropriate. In adults like ourselves and our parents, however, such behavior is disordered. An adult who refuses to repent of such behavior is stuck, unable to harvest the holy out of conflict because he will habitually mute any source of conflict, either between persons or the conflict he suffers within himself, that conflict of moral injury discussed earlier. Such adults, when faced with conflict, will hit the mute button, either by shutting down discussion through rage or self-pity, or by simply refusing to talk or listen at all.

Inner conflict is not of God and will not bring you peace. Conflict between people, however, can bring about peace. In his First Letter to Saint Timothy, Saint Paul uses the phrase "the good fight of faith" (1 Tm 6:12 — Douay-Rheims) to indicate that there are two ways of fighting: for our own glory or for the greater glory of God.

Only one of those brings about peace. Alas, that peace may not rise between you and an unrepentant sinner, but a fight fought for the glory of God will bring *you* peace *within the conflict itself* because, through prayer, study, and self-sacrifice, you have had the purity of your intention proven to you.

Interior peace gives us confident strength. A peacemaker, then, will not use any phrases from the list above to silence others. A peacemaker is secure in God's loving guidance that he can navigate through any conflict with another toward the destination — union with a loving God, who is all peace.

Peace Offerings

Peacemakers don't give in to self-pity. In order to make peace inside ourselves so deep that it has a chance of spreading to those around us, especially our families, we need to recognize the danger that is self-pity. The purpose for doing so is twofold, sort of threefold. First of all, when we see how self-pity undermines our own peace with God, we will be motivated to counter it with the basics already practiced through the earlier Beatitudes. Secondly, when we are able to identify self-pity in ourselves, we are able to protect ourselves from others weaponizing their own self-pity and using it to destroy our peace and our connection with Christ. That last bit serves us on two fronts. If we can spot the signs of self-pity in our children, we can correct them away from it, but we can only do so credibly if we're obviously fighting against it ourselves. In our relationships with unrepentant parents, we can identify self-pity at work in them so that we can protect ourselves and our children against it while still staying on the path to God's goodness.

I know that there is a lot of protestation against the word "victim" because it implies helplessness, whereas the term "survivor" implies strength in the face of insurmountable odds. "Survivor" is the word I use here far more often than "victim." That said, if there had been no case of victimization, there would have been nothing to survive in the first place. If you are reading this book, you suffered at least some injustice in your childhood that has in some way threatened the stability of your adult life and your children's emotional lives. You have suffered helplessness. Surviving that experience comes with a lot of temptation toward self-pity.

The danger in self-pity is that it keeps the focus on you and not on connecting with God through healthy relationships. All fractures in human relationships are a result of sin. Our broken relationships with our families are no exception. Granted, we survivors are not perfect just by virtue of having been victimized. If you have studied and prayed through all the previous chapters, hopefully your eyes have been opened to any places in your life where you may have legitimately sinned against others, even against the parents who have hurt you so badly. If you want peace in your soul, through the grace of God especially as dispensed in the Sacraments of Reconciliation and Eucharist, you can confront your own sinfulness in the relationship and begin making reparations — in other words, repairing the damage your sins have caused.

I spoke in the chapter on God's love about my own struggles with self-pity. When, in young adulthood, I discovered the depths of my parents' sins against me, I had to ask God, "Why didn't you protect me?" It was easy to feel sorry for myself, and it still is sometimes. I go online and see all these mommy bloggers with their beautifully cultivated Instagram accounts, sharing bright, shiny ideas of how to teach young children the Faith through liturgical snacking, and how to glorify God through interior decorating. Meanwhile, here I am trying to squelch down triggers that make me want to scream and scratch my squirmy kids off of me because they won't stop touching me when I want to be left alone. I just want a break sometimes and not to have to answer anyone else's demands that I once again care about them, when all the evidence indicates that nobody in the world really cares about me. Any energy I could have put into making a living room gallery wall of mid-century images of the Blessed

Mother just went into not yelling at my kids for something that was a completely pure and natural impulse for affection on their part.

I've cried out to God, "It's not fair!" The cry is not without truth. It *isn't* fair that my fight is with my past rather than the giclée print artist. However, the very fact that I have this fight at all is a sign of God's protection for me. If you're reading this book, it's a sign of God's active protection of you. *We have been lavishly protected from the idea that what was done to us was acceptable.* We have been protected plenty — protection not just for us but for future generations that spring from our wonderful, wounded, surviving lives. That is a far greater protection than not having suffered anything at all, for a lack of suffering is no insurance against our own sin. For this, let us thank God together.

Incidentally, when we live at peace with ourselves and use that peace to wage war against self-pity, we provide a good example of Beatitude for our children. We also grow in habits that make it easier to make peace with our children when we fall back on bad habits of self-absorption. Dr. Craig Malkin, psychologist and lecturer at Harvard University, has done a lot of work on the topic of self-absorption — or narcissistic tendencies, as he would be more likely to say. In his book *Rethinking Narcissism: The Secret to Recognizing and Coping with Narcissists*, Dr. Malkin describes the difference between healthy narcissism, where a person exercises one's God-given right to matter to another person (if you doubt this, see Genesis 2:18, where God states pretty plainly, "It is not good for the man to be alone"), versus toxic narcissism, which uses self-centeredness as a way to overpower others and obliterate anyone's will but the narcissist's.[42]

Healthy family relationships nurture that healthy narcissism, especially when we freely address the hurts we've committed against our children. Those hurts, however, are all but inevitable in this fallen world. Dr. Malkin writes, "You can't get close enough

---

42. Craig Malkin, *Rethinking Narcissism: The Secret to Recognizing and Coping with Narcissists* (New York: HarperCollins, 2015), 54–55.

to touch someone without stepping on their toes ... We inevitably hurt the people we love. The key to happy relationships with our children — or with anyone, for that matter — isn't being perfect. It's having the courage to acknowledge when we screw up. That's repair work, and it's central to developing healthy narcissism." All it takes to reach for peace is a re-do. What's a re-do, according to Malkin? "You acknowledge the mistake and try again. If you teach your kids how to do that, they'll learn that mistakes are a part of closeness. Repair and love go hand in hand."[43]

Rupture/repair. Death and rising. Sin and redemption. The less acceptable we make it in our own lives to live with denial and self-pity, the less our children will tend toward it themselves and the more they will connect themselves to healthy relationships — including with you, the parent.

Just War
The sins wounding your relationship with your family of origin might not be yours, and like all sin, those wounds are rooted in the selfishness of the sinner(s) in question. While I discourage you from diagnosing your family of origin with psychological disorders (even if you're a trained, licensed therapist because so much closeness can blur even the most professional vision), there is much to be said for looking at selfish behavior through psychology's understanding of narcissism, from narcissistic personality traits all the way up to Narcissistic Personality Disorder.

Dr. Malkin offers this perspective and a wealth of practical tools, first for evaluating our relationships to help us determine if we are trying to build a relationship with a hurting person who just needs to — and probably can — break narcissistic habits, or if we are faced with someone who is entrenched in his unrepentance, someone the Bible calls "senseless, faithless, heartless, ruthless" (Rom 1:31). For our own sakes and the sakes of the souls we

---

43. Malkin, *Rethinking Narcissism*, 179.

seek to reach for God's glory, we would be wise to discern which types of sinners we are dealing with in our family of origin. Dr. Malkin has seen in his own research and practice that people with narcissistic tendencies may be capable of developing empathy, putting themselves in another's emotional shoes, which is the key to developing healthy relationships. These people often can learn to build relationships rather than maintain their own armor.[44]

In other words, some sinners, even in our families of origin, may be willing to repent of their self-pity and build a genuine, mutually beneficial connection with you. Hold out an olive branch, sometimes two, and they'll see the error of their ways and set about faithfully amending those errors, of engaging in rupture/repair.

That said, there is no guarantee that our families of origin ever will be willing to repent. Even Dr. Malkin, a secular psychologist, writes, "The people you love can't change if they're unwilling to acknowledge their problems."[45] If you want to go for healing your relationship with your family of origin, you will have to find out their level of willingness to acknowledge and work toward amending their problems. This can be done by talking gently but honestly about your pain, usually with the support of a well-trained therapist. If your bid for connection with your family of origin is met with genuine sorrow, repentance, and reparation for sin, then heaven rejoices! The road to healing may be long, but there's no reason it cannot be traveled. Best of all, the journey ends at heaven for all who walk it!

If, however, your offer of Beatitude is met with cries of self-pity, such as rage at the injustice of your "false accusations," protests that you are the one victimizing your parent, or with stonewalling silence, then you have your answer. The dry land on which you could build a relationship with your family of origin remains

---

44. Ibid., 117–130.
45. Ibid., 119.

204 *Blessed Are the Peacemakers*

covered in the waters of self-pity. If you have done all you could to offer peace — acknowledged their sin, given them a chance to repent, and you did not mute them — then you have honored their gift of free will. You may be wise to make peace by limiting or ending contact with any family member who reacts thusly. The Church advises us through Saint Paul, "*If possible, on your part*, live at peace with all" (Rom 12:18, emphasis mine). After all, even Jesus wasn't able to live at peace with all, and that was through no fault of his! Yet by giving people the opportunity to accept but fail his peace, Jesus redeemed any suffering any of us may meet in the name of making peace. We read in Colossians 1:20 that Jesus made peace by the blood of the cross. Facing our family's rejection of our peacemaking may be the cross God has chosen for us. Praised be his name.

A Separate Peace

The people who've hurt us are human and on some level are affected by having hurt you and are terrified of what they let themselves become. This is not to cause us to write off what they did, but this is to make it clear that letting them get away with what they did will not bring them peace either. Until they face what they did and accept the consequences without defense, denial, or minimization, they will always have to run from all the ways they have damaged their own souls. They'll run through blame-shifting, competition, bad-mouthing, minimizing … I could go on and on. They do these things because they feel guilt, and they're terrified of the work they need to do to actually and effectively assuage that guilt. They are seeking appeasement when what they really want is absolution. Appeasement will not bring them peace.

In its section on the Fourth Commandment, "Honor Your Father and Mother," the *Catechism* talks about parental duties and even touches, if obliquely, on what should happen when parents fail those duties. In a section titled "The Family and the Kingdom," we read:

> Family ties are important but not absolute. Just as the child grows to maturity and human and spiritual autonomy, so his unique vocation which comes from God asserts itself more clearly and forcefully. Parents should respect this call and encourage their children to follow it. They must be convinced that the first vocation of the Christian is to follow Jesus. ... Becoming a disciple of Jesus means accepting the invitation to belong to God's family, to live in conformity with His way of life. (2232–33)

When parents fail to provide this respect, the Church is to be the sanctuary that God leaves for his people whose families fail them. Saint John Paul II writes in *Familiaris Consortio,* "For those who have no natural family the doors of the great family which is the Church — the Church which finds concrete expression in the diocesan and the parish family, in ecclesial basic communities and in movements of the apostolate — must be opened even wider. No one is without a family in this world: the Church is a home and family for everyone, especially those who 'labor and are heavy laden' (Mt 11:28)."[46]

We are not left orphans. Jesus made the Church our Mother for a reason. He knew we'd need it, some of us more than others.

Holy War

Peacemaking comes after justice, mercy, and purity of heart for a reason. Once we use those Beatitudes to reach inner peace, we can relate to others with transparency. Transparency in relationships with both self and others means that you have nothing to hide. Ask any addict in recovery about the anxiety that comes

---

46. John Paul II, *Familiaris Consortio,* par. 85.

with hiding and you'll get an earful. Ask Adam and Eve in the garden how it feels to have to hide from God, the all-seeing. Anybody with something to hide can never know peace. It follows, then, that if you live so that you have nothing to hide, you will be at peace. That's the freedom that comes with making peace and living a transparent life.

In cultivating the freedom that comes with transparency, peacemaking starts by recognizing what destroys peace, perhaps more than any other Beatitude basic. We no longer have anything to hide from ourselves, so there's no longer any point in trying to hide our true selves from others — including possibly our unrepentant parents. Peacemakers have embraced all the earlier Beatitudes and now can relate to their children from a place of honest transparency, but one tempered with good boundaries that honor a child's developmental needs. A transparent parent knows by God's guidance what to share with their children and when, in order to build relationship without oversharing, keeping the honesty child-focused rather than parental self-pity focused. Transparency at its heart is not about being the focus of a child's shock and awe. Rather, it is about the peace that comes from letting our children see us humble in our sinfulness and our efforts to strive for heaven.

Peacemakers are at peace with themselves because they set boundaries around their path to heaven. Peacemakers invite others, especially their children, to walk with them to heaven, even if their paths are surprising. Peacemakers know right from wrong, but that does not mean they won't face holy conflict. This is because peacemakers do not tolerate sin. Just like our first parents Adam and Eve, we fallen humans are drawn to sin. Worse, we are drawn to hide our sin from those we love and especially from ourselves. We are prone to power grabs and denial, to adding sin upon sin, kidding ourselves. When sin and denial of sin become habitual, our ability to connect with others, our own consciences, and with our loving God become terribly compromised. In children, this is immaturity and is to be expected, even if it needs be a subject for correction and instruction. In adults, this type of deep pattern of denial is disorder. That spiritual work of mercy "admonish the sinner" takes on a difficult timbre when the admonishment comes from an adult child pointing out her own parent's failings. If you want peace, you must become sin-intolerant because where there is sin, there is naturally conflict between what the sinner selfishly desires and the image of a perfect God stamped on that sinner, body and soul.

Becoming sin-intolerant is no small feat for anyone, but it looms especially large in relationships with the types of habitual sinners who are your average dysfunctional parents. Alas, sometimes peacemaking may look like cutting off contact with destructive family members. Jesus only got crucified the one time, after all. However, there's no point avoiding the fact that his peacemaking did get him crucified. Of course, his crucifixion also got him resurrected. His faith in the Father's good will for him empowered him to face the ultimate persecution. Yes, Jesus is divine, but he is also human, and even a human can grow secure in the knowledge that God will make all things right and all things new. This is why, even before he had experienced his resurrection, he held out hope to all of us that there is blessing for those persecuted for the sake of what's right.

HOLY FAMILY MOMENT
"Here Are My Mother and Brothers." (Mt 12:46–50)
Family is so integral to our identity as human beings that Jesus made sure we'd always have one available through him. Whoever does his heavenly Father's will is family with him. This is such a consolation when the families who could have loved us and been there for us instead chose selfishness, cowardice, and

self-comfort. When we live for truth instead of earthly appeasement, we are guaranteed the peace that comes with belonging to
an eternal family. When we reach out in new places — church
groups, close friendships, secular support groups — that is when
we meet our true family in Christ.

BEATITUDE BASIC WORKSHOP
Transparency

1. Practice listening to conflict, both external and internal, without automatically reaching for the mute
button. Ask God to show you what he might want
you to learn about his love through the experience
of this conflict. If sitting with these big feelings seems
unbearable, seek trusted counsel on how to develop
this skill.

2. Fight the good fight against self-pity: In your journal,
make a list of ways and times that God has protected
you and led you closer to his love. Perform the same
exercise for your children and even for your parents.

3. Prayerfully consider how true peacemaking should
shape your relationship with your children and parents. Ask God to show you how he wants you to
approach your parents, especially with an attitude
of Beatitude. How might their reactions shape the
boundaries you set between yourself, your children,
and them? Journal your answers.

AN ACT OF CONTRITION

I received this on a prayer card at a retreat for lay Dominicans, and
it remains my favorite Act of Contrition. I find it especially useful
as a survivor of family abuse because it includes any sins of which

I may not be cognizant.

Forgive me my sins, O Lord, forgive me my sins;
The sins of my youth, the sins of my age,
The sins of my soul, the sins of my body,
My idle sins, my serious voluntary sins,
The sins I know, the sins I do not know;
The sins I have concealed so long, and which are now hidden from
    my memory.
I am truly sorry for every sin, mortal and venial, for all the sins of
    my childhood up to the present hour.
I know my sins have wounded thy tender Heart, O my Savior,
Let me be freed from the bonds of evil through the most bitter
    passion of my redeemer.
Amen.
O my Jesus, forget and forgive what I have been.
Amen.

SAINT-SPIRATION
Saint Dymphna

Saint Dymphna was the Christian daughter of a pagan Irish king in the days before Christianity was widespread across that island. She was the spitting image of her mother, and when her mother died, the king was distraught. When he asked his courtiers for a solution to his heartbreak, they suggested he marry a girl who resembled his first wife. That girl was Dymphna.

Now that it was clear that her family was not a safe place for her, Dymphna looked to her faith for help. Her priest helped her escape across sea and land to the town of Gheel, Belgium, but it was not long before Dymphna's father tracked them down even there. The king continued to beg Dymphna to be his wife, but when she proved unrelenting, he himself murdered his own daughter in a fit of rage.

The story does not end with death, however. As time went on, visitors to Dymphna's tomb found themselves recovering from illnesses, especially illnesses of the mind and heart. Today she is the patron of the mentally ill as well as victims of incest. Saint Dymphna is one who stood her ground against the worst kinds of betrayal from one who was supposed to give her peace and safety, not rob her of both. When those who are supposed to be sanctuary for us instead want unholy appeasement and gratification, Saint Dymphna shows the way toward true peace.[47]

47. "Saint Dymphna," Catholic Online accessed February 17, 2020, https://www.catholic .org/saints/saint.php?saint_id=222. John Wasikowski, Nine Days with Saint Dymphna and Saint Gereban (John Wasikowski, 2014). Kindle.

— 10 —

BLESSED ARE THEY WHO ARE PERSECUTED FOR THE SAKE OF RIGHTEOUSNESS

For Theirs Is the Kingdom of Heaven

Beatitude Basic: Fortitude

In the LORD I take refuge;
how can you say to me,
"Flee like a bird to the mountains!
See how the wicked string their bows,
fit their arrows to the string
to shoot from the shadows at the upright of heart."

— Psalm 11:1–2

What's Wrong With This Picture?

I am a member of an online support group for Catholic women who strive to love rightly after having not experienced love from mother figures in their lives. I asked my support group sisters for some examples from their lives of what it was like to stand up to one's parents for the sake of something objectively good only to be punished for doing so.

> From Hailey*: When I was 12 years old, my mother told me and my 9-year-old sister that she was going to leave my father and move far away (she wouldn't say where) and that we could choose who we were going to live with. I told her that I was going to tell my father, and she immediately said that if I told him, she'd leave sooner, and if I didn't tell him, she'd think about staying. About a month later, she disappeared without any warning. We later found out that she had met someone online and moved across the country to live with him. Still to this day when I ask her why she abandoned us, she says that she gave me a chance to come, and I threatened to tell my Dad, so she knew she couldn't trust me. Also she says that she left because I never liked her and that my sisters and I fought too much and that we were making her miserable.
>
> From Michelle*: When I was about 15, I decided to take the TV out of my bedroom, so I'd have less distraction and not be tempted to watch trash. My dad got so upset. I don't remember what his reasons were, but I clearly remember him arguing with me about it.
>
> From Beatrice*: When I was about 7, my brother carved my name into the banister. My parents would not even

entertain the idea that it was not me. I cried and begged, and they withheld privileges until I would admit it. When the threat of a rare chance to go to the pool came up, I finally "admitted" what they wanted to hear. It killed me. About a week later, my brother was caught writing my name on the bathroom wall. I was then punished for lying previously in my fake confession.

From Theresa*: When I was 18 or 19, I took my cousin to DC. A hurricane hit, and somehow my mom manipulated me to drive through it to get "safely" home (a five-hour drive). I tried to fight her on it, but I was still young and brainwashed: "mother knows best." My cousin and I now look back on it and realize how she put our lives in danger.

You probably have several similar examples of your own. We shouldn't need a book to tell us that a parent is supposed to show her child right from wrong. When parents punish children for actually doing right, we know there is something wrong. Yet aren't parents supposed to correct their children? Aren't children who resist correction the ones in the wrong? And doesn't the Church, through the Bible and the *Catechism*, warn us that children who fail to respect and honor their parents, even when those children are adults themselves, are failing God's design for a good and holy family? Aren't adult children who turn their backs on their parents committing grave sin?

Those questions are all worth asking. God does want us to honor and respect our parents. Ignoring that aspect of God's will does mean death. However, when parents seek to harm their children because their children want to please God rather than appease their parents' boundaryless demands, this constitutes a double betrayal. Jesus sees our conflict and our sufferings at the hands of unrepentant parents, and if we persevere through the crosses with which they burden us, he promises us blessings. He definitely promises blessings on our children. I like to think he even promises blessings on our dysfunctional families of origin.

Let's face another fact: Even if we miraculously threw off our own tendency to sin and suddenly guided our children with perfect goodness, our kids would still be likely to fight against our efforts to guide them. So between both our own parents and those children to whom we are parents, we are in double need of every blessing that gets shed upon those persecuted for the sake of righteousness. Let's look at those blessings now and how God wills such blessings over our fallen human families.

Déjà Vu All Over Again

"Blessed are they who are persecuted for the sake of righteousness, for theirs is the kingdom of heaven" (Mt 5:10). Okay, class, time for a pop quiz: Which part of that verse sounds really familiar? If you guessed, "Theirs is the kingdom of heaven," you're right. This is the exact same blessing promised to the poor in spirit, or those who have packed their parenting pantries with teachability. By now you know that we can be pretty confident that Jesus never repeats himself without good reason. In attaching this blessing to both the very first Beatitude and the very last, Jesus is telling us something huge.

It's worth reviewing what exactly is this "kingdom of heaven." Is it simply heaven, and we have to work our way there by being good? It can't be simply that because in Luke 17:21, Jesus also tells us that "the kingdom of God is among you." So the kingdom of God, the kingdom of heaven, isn't something for which we must wait. This kingdom can be present in the here and now. The New American Bible, Revised Edition offers this commentary on Matthew 3:2, where John the Baptist first tells the people, "Repent, for the kingdom of heaven is at hand," that, "The expression 'the kingdom of heaven' ... means the effective rule of God over his people. In its fullness it includes not only human obedience to God's word, but the triumph of God over physical evils, supremely over death."[48]

For both the poor in spirit and those persecuted for the sake of righteousness, possessing the kingdom of heaven means an ownership in a state of being where people are ruled not by their frail whims and disordered desires but by the firm and gentle hand of the God who loves each of us into being. Dying in communion with Christ will transport us wholly into that kingdom. When Jesus comes again in glory at the judgment, we will get the full manifestation of God's kingdom over the new heavens and the new earth. However, we don't need to die or to have Jesus come back to possess God's kingdom. When we live the Beatitudes, Jesus promises us his kingdom even here, even now, even in the midst of great suffering.

Of course, the kingdom of heaven is a pearl of great price, a price Jesus paid with his blood. We too must not count the cost. We must connect deeply with Christ in order to live as he desires us to do. This is the heart of fortitude, that virtue that helps us endure that which we could never endure without Jesus making us new in him. Where Jesus is, so is the kingdom, and so is the resurrection — but first the cross.

Good Company

I realize I'm repeating myself here, but it bears repeating: Family dysfunction is caused not by a generational dynamic of habitual abuse nor by any wider cultural climate; family dysfunction is caused by personal sin and an aversion to holiness. Thus serving your family of origin as well as your own children with truth and meekness will very likely make some of them angry, espe-

---

48. Confraternity of Christian Doctrine, Matthew 3:2, in the New American Bible, Revised Edition (Washington: Confraternity of Christian Doctrine, 2010), bible.usccb.org/bible/matthew/3.

cially those who aren't yet inwardly disposed toward the pursuit of holiness. It bears repeating why. In children, including the ones you are raising, this is immaturity, and a certain level of immaturity is completely appropriate in children as they grow. In adults, including the ones who raised you, however, this is disorder. Of course, if you know your Bible, you know that Jesus handled more than anyone's fair share of adults mired in their own disordered thinking. The Pharisees, Sadducees, priests, and scribes, all the way down to the Rich Young Man and Judas Iscariot: they were so afraid of truth that when the truth stood in front of them and offered them unconditional love in the person of Jesus Christ, they walked away. They betrayed him. They mocked him. They beat him and stripped him naked. They crucified him.

That's how much the truth scares some people. Jesus experienced persecution whenever he told the truth. We can expect no better for ourselves, not from our children who are still growing in mind and heart, and alas, not even from our families of origin. Wherever there is truth in this fallen world, the fallen world will try to kill it because the very nature of the Fall is death. Thankfully, we are not without divine reassurance that all will be made new. In Romans 8, Saint Paul assures us that, as much as we can expect persecution from anyone uncomfortable with the truth, we can also expect support and vindication from God himself. Pay special attention to verses 31–33, where Paul exhorts us, "What then shall we say to this? If God is for us, who can be against us? He who did not spare his own Son but handed him over for us all, how will he not also give us everything else along with him? Who will bring a charge against God's chosen ones? It is God who acquits us."

Acquittal means freedom and redemption from punishment. When, through the gift of fortitude, we stand up for righteousness in the faces of people who wish we wouldn't, we are freed from slavery to the poor earthly comfort that comes from denying one's conscience. This, after all, is the pain of moral injury about which we spoke in previous chapters. Moral injury unhealed keeps us imprisoned in a war of our own continuing. In his love, Christ wants us free from that war. That said, we must be careful to examine the roots of our pain, to make sure our suffering is, in fact, for the sake of righteousness and not in service of our own denial. In the face of pain, how can we be sure that we are being persecuted by sinners and not corrected by a just and loving God?

As we saw in our chapter on comfort for the mourning, where we examined how God honors and expands on truthful emotional connection, pain tells us something. It's the gift of fortitude that empowers us to listen long enough to hear what pain is saying. That fortitude is what marks us as mature followers of Christ. If we have let our meekness become weakness, we will be disinclined to honor the boundaries between ourselves and the choices, desires, emotions, and needs of others. In this case, we will be drawn into sin by trying to dominate others through blasting them with our wants and feelings, as if they were responsible for making things right for us. The meek person will act with fortitude and feel his own pain; the weak person will demand that another make him feel better right now, in a sort of adult temper-tantrum: rage, sulking, withdrawal, up to and including physical and sexual violence. The person who forgets the value of emotional truth and boundaries cannot help but fall into injustice, stubbornness, distraction from the good, and an eventual inner turmoil that can only be made calm by crying out to God with a repentant heart, "Lord, save us! We are perishing!" (Mt 8:25)

In case you don't recognize that last quote, it's from when Jesus was asleep in the boat, and a storm came upon him and his disciples. Before he calmed the storm, however, he says something to his frightened shipmates, something that might sound callous and mocking — persecuting rather than guiding, if you will — if not seen in the light of God's love. Jesus says, "Why are you terrified?" (Mt 8:26) With this question, Jesus isn't shaming us for our feelings, as I, as a survivor of family abuse and dysfunction, used to think he was. No, he is asking us to ask ourselves why we are terrified. *He wants us to connect with our emotions.* And in sleeping, he invites us to look at the roots of his emotions. Why wasn't he terrified in this story? Because he knew that, whatever happened to him, especially things out of his human control, were willed by the Father. He did not fear death because he saw even earthly death as a way God expresses his love for us. Jesus is pure of heart. Jesus is gratitude, even in the storm. Jesus, knowing the role of the gift of fortitude, could sleep even through a hurricane.

We must make a practice of honestly reviewing our thoughts and actions, actively searching out sins to be conquered and virtues to be nurtured. Go through the Two Greatest Commandments and the other Beatitudes in order to make sure you're actually suffering for the sake of the truth and not just because you're not getting your way. Ask God to give you sincerity of heart. Be like David and ask God to judge you. See 1 Peter 4, especially verses 14–15, which tell us, "If you are insulted for the name of Christ, blessed are you, for the Spirit of glory and of God rests upon you. But let no one among you be made to suffer as a murderer, a thief, an evildoer, or as an intriguer."

Another marker of your own fortitude will be in the fruits of your actions.

> Beware of false prophets, who come to you in sheep's clothing, but underneath are ravenous wolves. By their fruits you will know them. Do people pick grapes from thornbushes, or figs from thistles? Just so, every good tree bears good fruit, and a rotten tree bears bad fruit. A good tree cannot bear bad fruit, nor can a rotten tree bear good

fruit. Every tree that does not bear good fruit will be cut down and thrown into the fire. So by their fruits you will know them. (Matthew 7:15–20)

Remember God's mercy: The merciful, which means the repentant, need have no fear of judgment.

Tough Love

Once we get in the habit of seeing our own sins clearly, two things happen. First, we become sensitized to our own sins. They bother us enough that we want to stop committing so darned many of them. Secondly, however, we see others' sins in a whole new light. This tends to shed light in two seemingly opposite but closely related directions. An overall sensitivity to sin in general opens our eyes to others' weaknesses; in other words, once we see how hard a time we have in conquering especially habitual sins, we have a better understanding of the uphill climb our fellow fallen humans face in just confronting, let alone turning away from, their own sins. This gives us the ability to exercise God's mercy toward others and ourselves.

That said, once we've had our own measure of success in turning away from sin, we have proof positive of our own free will. We have experienced that sin is something to which we can say, "No." Thus we must admit that others' sins against us are not accidents, are not incidents of their own victimhood getting away with them. We are free to see the painful truth that their sins against us are acts of will, chosen failures of their fortitude. Many an adult recovering from childhood abuse is surprised to discover the depths of dysfunction in which she was raised — which she still may be facing in her current relationship with her parents. Throw grandchildren into the mix, whose innocence parents have a duty to safeguard, and we can see how difficult it becomes to live in the tension between honoring our parents and serving our children.

Perhaps you even have experience with a parent who uses Church teaching to pressure you into appeasing sinful demands. That kind of pressure fills the good-willed child with great doubt. Sirach 3 is all about the agony that waits for those children who don't honor their fathers and respect their mothers. Some of that chapter's greatest hits? "For the Lord sets a father in honor over his children and confirms a mother's authority over her sons. Those who honor their father atone for sins; they store up riches who respect their mother" (Sir 3:2–4). "Those who fear the Lord honor their father, and serve their parents as masters" (Sir 3:7). "Kindness to a father will not be forgotten; it will serve as a sin offering — it will take lasting root" (Sir 3:14).

This isn't just Old Testament stuff either. Jesus himself warns the Pharisees against withholding material support for their parents and claiming that it's because that money is dedicated to God (see Mk 7:11–12). The *Catechism* tells us, "As they grow up, children should continue to respect their parents. They should anticipate their wishes, willingly seek their advice, and accept their just admonitions. Obedience toward parents ceases with the emancipation of the children; not so respect, which is always owed to them." (2217).

Christ, however, also uses his Church to counsel us prudently in the face of our doubts. In fact, God barely makes us turn the page from the above verses and quotes before doing so. I like to think that's because he remembers how weary we are. If you read just a few verses down in Sirach, you'll read, "A stubborn heart will have many a hurt; adding sin to sin is madness. When the proud are afflicted, there is no cure; for they are offshoots of an evil plant" (Sir 3:27–28). Just after Jesus points out the Pharisees' hypocrisy, he calls out the distortion of God's goodness at its root by saying, "You nullify the word of God in favor of your tradition that you have handed on" (Mk 7:13). The *Catechism* also plainly states that, *before* children have duties to their parents, *parents have duties to their children.* "Parents must regard their children as children of God and respect them as human persons. Showing themselves obedient to the will of the Father in heaven, they educate their children to fulfill God's law" (2222).

God wants us to honor, respect, or support that which is *good*. It is against his nature to demand we honor insistence on the performance of evil, especially from hearts turned resolutely away from his love. So how do we honor a parent with a stubborn heart? How do we respect someone whose choices are based not out of love but foolish pride? How do we show God's mercy, which is reserved only for the repentant, but still honor the father or mother who refuses to repent?

We honor free will by presenting our parents with healthy choices. We respect free will by enforcing boundaries when those choices endanger us, our marriages, our children, our parents themselves. To do so takes holy endurance — fortitude. What do we do when our parents choose sin rather than love? We respect and honor them by praying that the Lord will reach them and show them the freedom that is repentance. We support them by showing them a good example in spite of their false teaching. We do not, however, give in to evil, not ever, not even from our own parents. Through the gift of fortitude, God frees us from the rule of sinful tyranny and keeps us under his lordship, giving us his kingdom.

It may seem like Jesus is asleep in the boat while our parents are throwing their storms at us. We can give our doubts to him. When he calms the storm, there is great calm.

What to Expect When You're Expecting Persecution

Once we have examined our well-formed consciences for any sin between ourselves and our parents (or our children, as the case may be), we must dig out any doubts we have and present them clearly to Jesus. If through thoughtful prayer you have decided that you need to set some kind of family boundary to protect meekness — either your own or someone else's — you can fully expect to get some kind of pushback from the person whose sleeping conscience is irritated by that boundary. If that person is your child, especially a dependent child, pushback is a rather natural part of the process of being a human still maturing in both mind and soul; testing your boundaries as a parent is part of the child's process of discovering himself as separate from you, a unique soul with independent meekness. Such conflict can be painful, but it always is fruitful when undertaken with an attitude of Beatitude.

I also encourage you to recognize some pitfalls to which survivors of family abuse are particularly prone, especially in relationships with their own children. As someone raised by parents who were not teachable and had poor boundaries, you may feel triggered during a conflict with your child and may be inclined to use whatever immature survival mechanism helped you get through being raised by your own parents. You may want to hide from a yelling child. You may want to yell back. You may want to hit back at a child who has hit you. You may want to let a withdrawn child stay withdrawn because you might find some temporary relief in the lie that silence means there is no conflict. You may be tempted to fall into people-pleasing, giving in to a child's immature demands just so you can get the conflict over with. Of course, none of these things actually resolve conflict. They just postpone it. Your child's rebellion is just another part of his fallen humanity, just as your unhealthy defensive habits are a part of yours. Go back and work your way through the earlier chapters to see where you can add more Beatitude Basics into your parenting practices. This also is a place where work with a well-qualified mental health professional can help you learn more godly, gently courageous parenting choices.

When it comes to expecting persecution from your parents at

any strides you make toward greater mental and spiritual health, the game is a bit different. Our children are working on maturity, but abusive and dysfunctional parents have surrendered that maturity in the name of false comfort. If they are entrenched in sin, they are almost by definition entrenched in denial. Denial is just another word for darkness. Jesus himself tells us, "For everyone who does wicked things hates the light and does not come toward the light, so that his works might not be exposed. But whoever lives the truth comes to the light, so that his works may be clearly seen as done in God" (Jn 3:20–21).

Jesus is not surprised by denial. Neither should we be. There's a reason that when we see a vampire on TV or in a movie, when that vampire is exposed to light, the vampire hisses, fights back, and sometimes even smolders. Art imitates life (*Twilight* excepted, I suppose, as my editor reminds me). Vampires are just a type representing the real flesh and blood humans we all know who drain others of life in order to make themselves feel temporarily better — to keep themselves effectually dead. In the light, vampires become dust. They'd rather survive by killing others than sacrifice themselves so that others may live freely. If in setting boundaries you ask an emotional vampire to come into the light, that person will fight you and fight hard for his perceived right to stay in the darkness.

Such people resist others' healthy boundaries because to do so requires they surrender control. Such loss of perceived control feels to them for all the world like they are the ones being persecuted, but it is only the pain of their consciences telling them things they'd rather not hear. Have empathy for such people. They are enslaved by their desires to keep others enslaved with them. They are disabled by their moral injury. They are hurting.

Empathize with them, but do not appease them. Through teachability and emotional connection, acquire the truth. Build for yourself godly boundaries that serve God's justice and not disordered human whims. Practice gratitude and transparency in all you do and experience the freedom God has ached you to live from the first breath he instilled into Adam's core. Do all in your power to please Jesus, who never takes from you without giving more than you ever could, who gave his life so that you could live with him in eternal joy and true comfort-connection. Fortitude will help you withstand all anyone could do to demand you give in. Let God renew your strength.

When you make the first seven Beatitudes a part of your relationships, especially with the people who do not want you to be free, you will be free indeed to withstand whatever persecution your betrayers may pour out upon you. You will no longer fear the cross God has permitted them to put in your lives, because in bearing that cross freely for all to see, their sins will be brought into the light. In facing your persecution with Jesus at your side, you expose your abusers. "Therefore do not be afraid of them. Nothing is concealed that will not be revealed, nor secret that will not be known" (Mt 10:26).

The First of Thousands
An abusive family may hate you for exposing their sin, for shining light into the darkness they so crave. They will very likely try to punish you for showing them the truth. Doing God's will in front of others who'd rather you didn't? That's tough stuff — tough stuff only fortitude can endure. Throughout salvation history, God promises the glory of his love to those who refuse to count the cost and stay with him in truth. He starts this promise with the very first of the Ten Commandments. He tells us to put him first (as, to be fair, he puts us first among all his creation). He tells us to have no other gods. "You shall not bow down before them or serve them. For I, the LORD, your God, am a jealous God, bringing punishment for their parents' wickedness on the children of those who hate me, down

to the third and fourth generation, but showing love down to the thousandth generation of those who love me and keep my commandments" (Dt 5:9–10).

How does this relate to our relationships with abusive parents? Unrepentant parents demand that we make them our gods. They are not, and the real God is not pleased when any human tries to usurp his authority over and love for us. When we set boundaries in anticipation of the likely sins of habitual sinners, we aren't being cruel or untrusting. We are imaging the God who makes clear consequences, both earthly and eternal, for the stiff-necked sinner. Psalm 69 is all about this kind of betrayal of both God and the family. We especially see this pain in verses 8–10.

> For it is on your account I bear insult,
>   that disgrace covers my face.
> I have become an outcast to my kindred,
>   a stranger to my mother's children.
> Because zeal for your house has consumed me,
>   I am scorned by those who scorn you.

Later, Jesus walked among us and told us that we should expect persecution for following him — persecution even from our own families. The entire chapter of Matthew 10 is dedicated to this. Especially poignant is Matthew 10:37, where Jesus tells us, "Whoever loves father or mother more than me is not worthy of me, and whoever loves son or daughter more than me is not worthy of me." Jesus anticipates this conflict between the child who wants to do God's will and the parent who wants the child to appease disordered whims.

Jesus anticipates our pain, but he also anticipates the chance this pain gives for rebirth, not just to the adult recovering in Christ's love from childhood abuse, but also for the abusers themselves, for whom hope may seem impossible. We must never forget that those abusers also are God's beloved creatures. Their failings rend his heart clean through. This is why even he who knows our ends before we begin still holds out hope for even the worst of sinners, the most habitual of abusers. Partnered with each of these places where God speaks of how sin tears families apart, we see another verse, just hiding in the warning's shadow, promising rescue when redemption comes at last.

- Whoever receives you receives me, and whoever receives me receives the one who sent me (see Mt 10:40).
- See, you lowly ones, and be glad;
  you who seek God, take heart!
  For the LORD hears the poor,
  and does not spurn those in bondage (Ps 69:33–34).
- [I show] love down to the thousandth generation of those who love me and keep my commandments (Dt 5:10).

Fortitude is what frees us to suffer through what it takes to establish physical, emotional, and spiritual protection for yourself and your children. This may, in fact, be just what your abusers need to show them their own need of repentance and mercy. If they do recognize it, and they do repent, then God is eager to bless them, even more eager than you could possibly be to have a parent who loves you with the selflessness you deserve through rupture/repair. Our standing up for God's truth in the face of injustice from our parents may be just like how Esther was put in a position to advocate for the rescue of her people. She was a pure-hearted girl brought into a corrupt court. She did not give in to that corruption. She was sorely tempted to turn her back on the threat of destruction of her kindred, but her uncle reminded her that to do so would only postpone the death of her and her whole family; cowering under threat would not deliver them. Rather, she leaned on her uncle's faith that God was somehow going to deliver their kin from this evil. She trusted God and allowed him to use her to be that someone (see Est 4, especially 11–17).

A woman of fortitude, Esther chose to stand up for truth in the face of certain death. She did so. She was spared, she and her whole extended family. If you set peace terms with your family of origin, expect them to fight back. If they are not poor in spirit themselves, they will resist, perhaps violently, any insinuation that they themselves might be wrong. This is because they have not developed the strong sense of self-reality that comes from following the Two Greatest Commandments and the Beatitudes.

If the pushback from either your family of origin or your children causes you to start doubting yourself, you have options. Reread the previous chapters of this book. Talk to a therapist. Approach a trusted friend. Turn to faith-filled friends. If you don't have any, find some. (Look to the appendix for ideas on how to do this.) Take the same approach that Esther did, and ask faithful people of fortitude to fast and pray with you for deliverance from the kind of evil that obliterates generations. Above all, take your doubts back to prayer and the sacraments.

If you are in pain, connect with that pain. Find out if God is instructing you or sinners are persecuting you for reminding them of their sin. Often enough, it's both. Standing up to parents who want you to do evil — leave grandchildren with them when they haven't demonstrated competence of skill in or attitude toward caring for the helpless, for instance — can be difficult. Parents who are weak rather than meek will pressure you into letting them escape any earthly consequences of their sin. When you stand up to them in truth and charity, living all the Beatitudes before their eyes, they might deny it all they want, but they will be touched by God's goodness playing out in front of them through your choices. In doing so, you bring them the kingdom of heaven. Alas, it is theirs to accept or reject. Every time they get a taste of actual consequences for their actions, they get an opportunity to get right with God. "Whoever brings back a sinner from the error of his way will save his soul from death and will cover a multitude of sins" (Jas 5:20).

HOLY FAMILY MOMENT
The Crucifixion

Jesus gave the motherless a mother from the cross because he knew what it would be like to be deserted and betrayed by the people who should have been there for him. But who was there for both him and us? Mary, the perfect parent. Saint John, the best brother we could ask for. Jesus knew his people would suffer because he suffered. He still suffers out of love for us. Thus, through all these good gifts, in our own crosses, especially in family crosses, we are never alone.

BEATITUDE BASIC WORKSHOP
Fortitude

1. Journal about a time when you were punished for doing the right thing and connect with the emotions that memory gives you. Ask God to show you how he protected the gift of fortitude within you by allowing you this experience and unite that memory to Jesus' sufferings on the cross.

2. Prayerfully study the differences between the type of "honor and respect" being requested of you by the immature and disordered in your life, versus how God defines honor and respect. Journal about choices you

can make in your next interactions that show true
honor and respect and ask God to help you stay strong.

3. Examine your fears of conflict, especially with your
children and parents. Journal on the question that
Jesus asked the disciples in the storm: Why are you
terrified? What do the reasons behind your fear tell
you about the places where God longs to cultivate
fortitude in your life?

A PRAYER FOR PROTECTION
OF ONE'S CHILDREN[49]

Holy Mother Mary, by virtue of your divine motherhood you
have become mother of us all. I place the dear ones God has given
me under your loving protection. Be a protecting mother to my
children. Guard their bodies and keep their thoughts ever holy
in the sight of their creator and God. Guard their hearts and keep
them pure and strong and happy in the love of God. Guard always
their souls, and preserve in them faithfully the glorious image
of God they received in Baptism. Always, Mother, protect them
and keep them under your motherly care. Supply in your all-wise
motherhood for my poor human deficiencies and protect them
from all evil. Amen.

SAINT-SPIRATION
Saint Bernadette Soubirous

Our Lady of Lourdes is my go-to girl when it comes to needing
a mother who wants justice for her children. Her chosen messenger, Saint Bernadette, is my go-to girl for knowing where to
go when it looks like that justice isn't going to happen and for
knowing when to obey God over man.

---

49. A. Francis Coomes, *Mother's Manual*, 45–46.

We often hear that Saint Bernadette came from a poor but pious family who practiced the Faith well before Mary literally walked into their lives. What gets downplayed is that when Bernadette came home with the story that a beautiful lady had appeared to her in the cave down by the river, her mother assumed she was lying and punished Bernadette accordingly. This was far from the end of the pain Bernadette would face for standing up for the truth. Bernadette would be harassed by neighbors and police and doubted by her own parents. Through it all, and already suffering from asthma in the cold, humid climate of Lourdes, she accepted whatever the Lord sent her.

Saint Bernadette Soubirous, pray for us when we are persecuted, whether by our own bodies or by those who don't want us to speak the truth. [50]

---

50. Alban Butler, *Lives of the Saints for Every Day in the Year* (Rockford: TAN Books, 1995), 148–149.

CONCLUSION

Now to him who is able to accomplish far more than
all we ask or imagine, by the power at work within
us, to him be glory in the church and in Christ
Jesus to all generations, forever and ever. Amen.

— Ephesians 3:20–21

A Little Bit Better

One day, as our kids played together at a nearby park, I was chatting with my friend Terri*, telling her about this idea I had for a book for all those people who had survived abusive childhoods and wanted to have better relationships with their own children and, maybe, even their own parents. Her eyes lit up. She told me about her own mom, who had worked so hard to do a better job raising Terri and her siblings than had been done by Terri's rage-driven, alcoholic grandfather.

"It's like each generation can get a little better, go a little farther, than the last," I remember her saying.

As this book took shape, I recalled the park conversation

and asked Terri if she might feel comfortable helping me reach out to her mom for an interview about her experience breaking the cycle with her own family. After some prayer, Terri got back to me. She didn't really feel comfortable doing that.

She explained, somewhat hesitantly, "I don't think my mom really came out of it all that well."

"Oh!" I answered, a bit confused but mostly worried that I'd caused my friend pain. "I'm so sorry. I misunderstood." I hesitated before asking, "Maybe you're the one I should be interviewing?"

She pursed her lips in thought. "I'm not sure *I* came out of it all that well either."

I recognized the pain in her eyes that accompanied her admission. It was the pain I feel every time I realize that I've harmed my own children through my failures. I told her I admired her courage for admitting it out loud, both to me and to herself.

"It's like I said before, I think. Each generation gets a little better than the last," she said. "Sometimes it's just a little."

Back to the Future

If I really think about it, I began writing this book when I was in eighth grade. I didn't know it at the time. All I knew was that I was researching for my eighth-grade term paper on the topic of missing children. If you'll recall, it was the '80s. Faces on milk cartons were becoming a thing, and I was all but obsessed with some missing persons show on HBO (Google is not surrendering its name, alas, otherwise I'd gladly credit it). So when we had to write a term paper in order to graduate eighth grade, I did not surprise myself when I chose "missing children" as the topic.

I was, however, surprised at what I read in the books I gathered at my local library, thanks to suggestions from the good old card catalog with its long, wooden drawers filled with endless, fragrant index cards. I read about the horrible abuses abducted children experienced, sure. Then I read about the many common behaviors exhibited by those rare children who had been recovered post-abduction. These traumatized children didn't like to be touched. They raged for no apparent reason. They were withdrawn, hesitant to talk or invest in friendships. They were awkward with their peers. With adults, they were overly eager to please. My thirteen-year-old brain was not able to put it into words at the time, but somewhere inside of me the thoughts were connecting, twisting their fibers together into a coherent analysis of my lived experience.

I behaved like someone who had been traumatized.

In my innocence, I was confused. Surely my father's rages and my mother's obsession with my body weren't enough to traumatize someone, I thought. I reassured my young self that my parents were right: I was, as usual, making a big deal out of nothing.

I am confident that the Holy Spirit used that term paper to show me truth, to begin the slow, as-gentle-as-supernaturally-possible process of revealing to me that the reality my parents had been selling me all that time was false. For example, even as I told myself I was blowing things out of proportion and just identifying too closely with the missing children whose stories I'd read, this was the time of my life in which I finally stood up to my mother for what she had been doing to me, as I described in Chapter 1. It was years before I was able to look back with the eyes of a freedom nurtured by faith and think that I wasn't just *behaving* like someone who had been traumatized. I *had been* traumatized, legitimately and habitually by both of the adults to whom my nurturing had been entrusted.

God delights in each one of us. He delights in the unique ways he gets to reveal the depths of his love for us. For me, it seems, he's loved inviting me to write my way back to him and the truth of his deep love. My healing process has been slow and very likely will continue to be slow, but I credit that eighth-grade term paper with saving my life — my anxious, people-pleasing, fear-crushed life. Likewise, I credit this book for saving my parenting. Even after writing the missing children term paper, I had a long way to go. Likewise with this book.

My parenting still has a long way to go. A *long* way to go. But with both of these writing assignments, God has dropped into my lap huge chunks of awareness of how I've been hurt and hurting. Both are truth. Both are healing, not just for myself but for the people entrusted to me in some way. As I come to the end of this assignment, this stage of the journey with you, Reader, I hope we can together take a close look at our next possible steps in our relationships with our children, our parents, ourselves, and our God.

Taking Stock

Together we have taken a look at all the good, wholesome, nurturing, and healing ingredients God wants us to have in our parenting: confidence, compassion, teachability, emotional connection, boundaries, sensitivity of conscience, repentance, gratitude, transparency, and fortitude. If these ingredients are old news to you, and you already use them in your parenting, I hope reading about them in this guidebook makes you feel validated and less alone. For my part, as I wrote about these ingredients, my eyes were opened not just to how many ways they were missing from my own parents' choices, but I also saw more clearly the dark places in my own life where I've been holding on to expired, poisonous ingredients that really just need to be thrown out and replaced with all the good, simple things God wants me to have, not just for my children's sake, but also for my own and even for my parents'.

If, as you read, you felt the pain of light shining into the darker corners of your own sins, do take heart. We may be surprised by our own blindness. God is not.

> I will lead the blind on a way they do not know;
>> by paths they do not know I will guide them.
> I will turn darkness into light before them,
>> and make crooked ways straight.
> These are my promises:
>> I made them, I will not forsake them. (Isaiah 42:16)

If you are tempted to doubt that God will stay with you in spite of your failings, especially knowing that you have failed an innocent child who depended on you for safety and nurture, give that doubt a dose of faith in a God who loves to choose the weak to shame the strong. He loves to fill our emptiness, to have us close. "Who is blind but my servant, or deaf like the messenger I send? Who is blind like the one I restore, blind like the servant of the LORD?" (Is 42:19) I'm not using this to single out people who are literally visually or hearing impaired. I'm using these verses to remind us that we are all blind. We are all deaf. We are all lost. We are all lacking in sense and in need of restoration. How God longs to restore us! How God longs to make all things new!

It's never too late to break the cycle. Have you hurt the children you are still raising? As far as it is safe for them for you to do so, apologize. Become an even more dedicated student of healthy parenting and throw yourself into rejecting all your bad habits — from habits of action all the way down to habits of thought. If you are still in a season of actively raising dependent children, create new experiences for them where they can trust you to be safe and loving. Seek help from a trustworthy therapist who can guide you in truth. Is that a scary prospect? That's fine. God has promised that he won't forsake you as you learn to love the light. He certainly won't forsake your children.

What if your kids are all grown and flown? What if you now

realize that you have abused your child and are only now understanding why he is not close to you, doesn't want you around, has cut you out of his life? You can find peace even now. First, accept whatever the reality is, whether your relationship with your adult child is strained but still alive, or your child has blocked you from his life. Accept the circumstances and feel the pain. Ask God what he is teaching you in that pain. Get in touch with your conscience. If you feel yourself resisting that pain, find a trustworthy counselor to help you work your way into that truth. Confess your sins. Fast. Pray. Perform acts of penance.

Are there things you wish you could do for your children and grandchildren but can't because you made choices with consequences that will follow you until your dying day? Find other children and grandchildren whom you can help, if from a safe distance. Buy baby outfits for a local children's charity. Make a donation, however small, to the local homeless shelter — men and women who might have broken relationships with their parents too. Love is still love, even if it must be from a distance. Surrender your self-focus, which is what dug this pit for you in the first place. Above all, give the people you've broken to God. He can fix anything, even your sins, if only you'll let go and let him.

What about your relationship with your parents? Can that be healed? What if they have the truth told them compassionately and they still remain stiff-necked, refusing to repent? What if you've borne persecution from them for refusing to appease their sinful demands, and it seems there is just no reaching them? If you have received any healing at all from Jesus for the brokenness your parents caused you, all you can do is what he told the Gerasene demoniac, from whom Jesus cast a legion of spirits: he told him, "Go home to your family and announce to them all that the Lord in his pity has done for you" (Mk 5:19). We don't know if the man's family even listened to him. We do know that, in following Christ's command, he spread the news of Jesus to way more than his family, for in the next verse we read, "and all were amazed."

What if, through prayer and thoughtful choices, you realize you can no longer have a relationship with one or both parents without risking the good of your own soul or the innocence of your children? Or what if you feel like you just can't love them for all the pain they've caused you and perhaps your children? Or what if your abusive parents are already dead, and it feels for all the world like there's no restoring what they took from you with them to their graves? Feeling like all of this is impossible? It is — without God. With God, all things are possible.

This is why the Beatitudes are so important to the temporal and eternal survival of the person who grew up at the hands of unrepentant parents. We, who were raised to think that we only existed to satisfy the selfish whims of sinners, are freed when we invite the Beatitudes to come alive in our present choices. The *Catechism* promises us:

> The Beatitudes reveal the goal of human existence, the ultimate end of human acts: God calls us to his own beatitude. This vocation is addressed to each individual personally, but also to the Church as a whole, the new people made up of those who have accepted the promise and live from it in faith. (1719)

> Such beatitude surpasses the understanding and powers of man. It comes from an entirely free gift of God: whence it is called supernatural, as is the grace that disposes man to enter into the divine joy. (1722)

While some parents are teachable and some are unrepentant, every parent is fallen, including ourselves. Whatever our pain, Jesus can handle it. Not only is he strong enough to handle the truth of our imperfect love, he's also strong enough to love our parents for us and to love our children through us, even when we fail them. We need only ask him to show us the perfect goodness of *his* parenthood. As the *Catechism* puts it, "No one is father as God is Father" (239).

Looking Back (and Forward)

When I think back to all the people I've encountered in the preparation of this book, I am overawed with their courageous humility. I especially think back to the conversations I had with Terri, described at the top of this chapter. In Terri's courage and honesty, I see a generous glimpse of how God makes all things new specifically through healing from family abuse and dysfunction. Scour the Bible and Church documents all you like and you'll never find a promise from Jesus that we will be perfect this side of the veil. What he does promise is complete joy. "As the Father loves me, so I also love you. Remain in my love. If you keep my commandments, you will remain in my love, just as I have kept my Father's commandments and remain in his love. I have told you this so that my joy may be in you and your joy may be complete" (Jn 15:9–11). Christ promises us complete joy, even here, even now. Through triggers, disappointments, grief, and our own failures — through those struggles to stay compassionately present to our children, our parents, and ourselves — joy remains ours for the taking. As long as we unite to him in all the struggles blessed in the Beatitudes, we are guaranteed his lordship, his comfort and mercy, his loving gaze, his fatherhood over us, and great reward in heaven.

We, like Terri, can give Jesus our "just a little bit better," and Jesus turns our need into a complete loaves-and-fishes situation. He promises that "just a little" that, when given back to him, he always multiples beyond perfection. He takes our just a little and turns it into more than enough. That is how to raise a family with guaranteed joy.

Where we should have been given loving examples, we received examples of what not to do. Where we should have been nurtured, we were harmed. Where we should have been allowed to thrive, to repair after rupture, we were barely permitted to survive. Yet out of the devastation of family abuse and dysfunction, hope stirs in the new life we have been given in our new families, in the opportunities for joyful, sustaining relationship with our own children. It is so easy to predict that, given our backgrounds, we can only expect further destruction in our own parenting lives. It also was easy for the scientists in 1980 to predict that the slopes of Mount Saint Helens could only remain barren for years and years to come.

Jesus defies all expectations. He breaks all cycles. He makes all things new, and what's amazing is how he does so: through God's very design, created well before the destruction began. The lupines that took root in the ash of Mount Saint Helens only did so because God made them to carry bacteria on their roots that provided what the barren soil lacked. The gophers survived the blast because God made them to burrow as a matter of course. Christ would not have risen without the cross. In our death is our way to new life. God designed us not just to survive the blast zone but to fill it with his life. Rupture becomes repair. Destruction resurrects into joy.

Life grows from death at a rate no human can anticipate. That is how God's love works, my fellow cycle-breakers. When we still fail, he is still with us, still growing life within us and in our relationships with our children. Sometimes it is just a little, but God does great things with just a little.

It is my hope that, by this point, you see that there is so much yet to do in your life as a parent, but also there is so much that Christ already has done for you. It's also my hope that, in showing you what God has done for me and the other cycle-breakers on these pages, you can see all the pure joy God has in store for you, your children, and even your parents. You can see Jesus rose from death out of barren rock. Christ is life in, from, and through the blast zone. He truly does make all things new. By his grace, may he continue to do so for all of us.

RESOURCES

The following resources may be helpful to you as you work with God on being both the parent and the child he longs for you to be.

For Wounds from the Past
Forgiving Mother: A Marian Novena of Healing and Peace (Franciscan Media, 2017) by Marge Steinhage Fenelon.

Remembering God's Mercy: Redeem the Past and Free Yourself from Painful Memories (Ave Maria Press, 2016) and *My Peace I Give You: Healing Sexual Wounds With the Help of the Saints* (Ave Maria Press, 2012), both by Dawn Eden.

The Body Keeps the Score: Brain, Mind, and Body in the Healing of Trauma (Penguin Books, 2015) by Bessel van der Kolk, MD.

From Grief to Grace: The Journey from Tragedy to Triumph (Sophia Institute Press, 2016) by Jeannie Ewing.

Grieving: Inviting God Into My Pain (iUniverse, 2011) by J. Catherine Sherman, PhD.

Rethinking Narcissism: The Bad — and Surprising Good — About Feeling Special (Harper Perennial, 2016) by Dr. Craig Malkin.

Unleashed: How to Receive Everything the Holy Spirit Wants to Give You (Ave Maria Press, 2015) and *Fearless: Conquer Your Demons and Love with Abandon* (Ave Maria Press, 2016), both by Sonja Corbitt. Corbitt has a unique, empowering way of addressing the father wound in all of us.

For Parenting and Other Relationships in the Present
These books offer practical approaches on how to use the Beatitudes in relationships, both with your children and others. Please keep in mind that several of these are written from secular perspectives and may at times express approaches that conflict with a Catholic worldview.

Boundaries: When to Say Yes, When to Say No, to Take Control of Your Life (Zondervan, 1992) by Henry Cloud and John Townsend. Also see *Boundaries with Kids* (2001) and *Boundaries with Teens* (2006).

The Temperament God Gave Your Kids: Motivate, Discipline, and Love Your Children (Our Sunday Visitor, 2012) by Art and Laraine Bennett.

Building Better Families: A Practical Guide to Raising Amazing Children (Beacon Publishing, 2008) by Matthew Kelly.

Try Softer: A Fresh Approach to Move Us Out of Anxiety, Stress, and Survival Mode — and Into a Life of Connection and Joy (Tyndale Momentum, 2020) by Aundi Kolber.

Parenting from the Inside Out: How a Deeper Self-Understanding Can Help You Raise Children Who Thrive (TarcherPerigee, 2013) by Daniel J. Siegel and Mary Hartzell.

The Power of Validation: Arming Your Child Against Bullying, Peer Pressure, Addiction, Self-Harm, and Out-of-Control Emotions (New Harbinger Publications, 2011) by Karyn D. Hall and Melissa H. Cook.

The Heart of Parenting: Raising an Emotionally Intelligent Child (Simon & Shuster, 1997) by John Gottman, Ph.D, and Joan De-Claire.

Is That Me Yelling?: A Parent's Guide to Getting Your Kids to Cooperate Without Losing Your Cool (New Harbinger Publications, 2014) by Rona Renner, RN.

The Power of Showing Up: How Parental Presence Shapes Who Our Kids Become and How Their Brains Get Wired (Ballantine Books, 2020) by Daniel J. Siegel, MD and Tina Payne Bryson, PhD.

The Grown-Up's Guide to Teenage Humans: How to Decode Their Behavior, Develop Unshakable Trust, and Raise a Respectable Adult (Harper Wave, 2017) by Josh Shipp.

Healing Reads: Inspirational Fiction
These books tell stories that provide inspiration that, no matter how we have been wounded by our parents, we can choose God and truth above all falsehood, including the falsehood of poor self-worth.

The Living Water Series (Howard Books), biblical historical fiction by Stephanie Landsem. *The Well* (2013), *The Thief* (2014), and *The Tomb* (2015), all tell stories of Jesus bringing healing and redemption to people from broken families.

Stay with Me (Full Quiver Publishing, 2015) by Carolyn Astfalk tells the story of a young couple, Rebecca and Chris, who must find how to love truly and freely out of the shadow of Rebecca's controlling father's manipulations.

The Grace Crasher (CreateSpace, 2017) by Mara Faro. Fleeing her alcoholic father and codependent mother, Julia fakes being an evangelical Christian so that she can get an apartment near the guy of her dreams. The truth chases her down, however, and she learns how to turn to God for healing in the most unexpected ways.

Intermission (Candent Gate, 2016) by Serena Chase. Madeline Faith discovers that she is more than just the odd girl out in her family of successful athletes. Through a youthful romance that leads her to discover Christ, she also discovers that she was made for more than her mother's control.

Websites for Therapy, Healing, and Connection
Catholic Therapists (catholictherapists.com) offers a referral base of qualified Catholic therapists. Read participating therapists' profiles to find one who might be the right fit for your needs.

Pastoral Solutions Institute (catholiccounselors.com) offers a wide variety of resources and professional services (including tele-counseling) intended to help committed Catholics overcome problems like marital conflict, childrearing problems, depression, anxiety, stress, and the difficulties associated with major life transitions.

John Paul II Healing Center (jpiihealingcenter.org) promotes the following mission: to promote and inspire transformation in the heart of the Church, by healing and equipping God's people for the New Evangelization.

Catholic in Recovery (catholicinrecovery.com) offers support for people recovering from substance abuse and other unhealthy attachments, offering meetings in-person and online.

Pocket Rehab (getpocketrehab.com) is a secure mobile app that uses a multilayered support system to help people struggling with or directly/indirectly affected by addiction. Pocket Rehab offers 24/7 real-time recovery support and relapse prevention for its members for free through an online community of volunteer providers.

Restore the Glory (restoretheglorypodcast.com): Dr. Bob Schuchts and Jake Khym are Catholic therapists with over 50 years combined experience teaching and accompanying people into fuller life and freedom. In this podcast, they discuss the value of integrating mental health resources with Catholic spirituality.

Saint Dymphna's Playbook (https://www.grexly.com/st-dymphnasplaybook): Hosted by Tommy Tighe, a marriage and family therapist, husband, and father, Saint Dymphna's Playbook is a podcast about finding mental well-being as a Catholic with the help of community and the saints.

Erin McCole Cupp (erinmccolecupp.com) for an inspirational email newsletter as well as social media written to reach sinners on their walk through repentance and into real relationships.

BIBLIOGRAPHY

Aquinas, Thomas, *Summa Theologiae*, 2nd and rev. ed. Translated by Fathers of the English Dominican Province. New Advent, 2017. https://www.newadvent.org/summa/

Arroyo, Raymond. *Mother Angelica: The Remarkable Story of a Nun, Her Nerve, and a Network of Miracles.* New York: Doubleday, 2005.

Biography.com Editors. "Saint Thomas Aquinas Biography." The Biography.com website. Updated September 10, 2020. https://www.biography.com/religious-figure/saint-thomas-aquinas

Butler, Alban. *Lives of the Saints For Every Day In the Year.* Rockford: TAN Books, 1995.

The Catechism of the Catholic Church. 2nd ed. Vatican: Libreria Editrice Vaticana, 2012.

Cloud, Henry and John Townsend. *Boundaries: When to Say Yes, When to Say No, to Take Control of Your Life.* Grand Rapids: Zondervan, 1992.

Coomes, A. Francis. *Mother's Manual.* Brooklyn: William J. Hirten Co. Inc., 1973.

Corbitt, Sonja. "Healing the Father Wound." Recorded talk at the 2014 Diocese of Venice, Florida, Women's Conference. https://vimeo.com/89403016.

Dominican Sisters of Saint Cecelia. "Saint Martin de Porres." Accessed February 16, 2021. https://www.nashvilledominican.org/community/our-dominican-heritage/our-saints-and-blesseds/st-martin-de-porres/.

Eden, Dawn. *My Peace I Give You: Healing Sexual Wounds With the Help of the Saints.* Notre Dame: Ave Maria Press, 2012.

EWTN Global Catholic Television Network. "Mother Mary Angelica. EWTN.com. Accessed February 16, 2021. http://www.ewtn.com/motherangelica/works.asp.

Faustina Maria Pia. "Litany of Trust." Sisters of Life. Accessed February 16, 2021. https://sistersoflife.org/wp-content/uploads/2019/05/Mobile-Litany-of-Trust-English-1.pdf.

John Paul II. "Apostolic Journey to the United States of America, Holy Mass at the Capital Mall, Washington (homily)." October 7, 1979. Vatican: Libreria Editrice Vaticana.

———. *Familiaris Consortio.* Vatican: Libreria Editrice Vaticana, 1981.

———. *Letter to Families.* Vatican: Libreria Editrice Vaticana, 1994.

Kelly, Matthew. *Building Better Families: A Practical Guide to Raising Amazing Children.* Beacon Publishing, 2008.

Kolber, Aundi,. *Try Softer: A Fresh Approach to Move Us Out of Anxiety, Stress, and Survival Mode — and Into a Life of Connection and Joy.* Carol Stream: Tyndale Momentum, 2020.

Latham, Charles. *Step by Step: Looking at the New Testament Beatitudes Through the Old Testament Feasts.* Spring Hill: Holy Fire Publishing, 2005.

Law Nolte, Dorothy and Rachel Harris. *Children Learn What They Live: Parenting to Inspire Values.* New York: Workman Publishing, 1998.

Lefcourt, Herbert M. "Locus of Control" In *Encyclopedia of Psychology.* Edited by Alan E. Kazdin, 5:68-70. Washington: American Psychological Association and Oxford University Press, 2000.

Luke 17:3 Ministries. Accessed February 16, 2021. http://www.luke173ministries.org.

Malkin, Craig. *Rethinking Narcissism: The Bad — And Surprising Good — About Feeling Special.* New York: Harper Collins, 2015.

Mary Perpetua. "Blessed Margaret of Castello." Catholicism.org. Accessed February 16, 2021. http://catholicism.org/blessed-margaret-castello.html.

Mongin, Helene. *The Extraordinary Parents of Saint Therese of Lisieux.* Translated by Marsha Daigle-Williamson. Huntington: Our Sunday Visitor, 2015.

Mount Saint Helens: Back From the Dead. Directed by Nick Davidson. Boston: WGBH, 2010.

Nakashima Brock, Rita and Gabriella Lettini. *Soul Repair: Recovering from Moral Injury After War.* Boston: Beacon Press, 2012.

O'Neel, Brian. *39 New Saints You Should Know.* Cincinnati: Servant, 2010.

Treasures of the Church. "The Murder." The Pilgrimage of Mercy: Tour of the Major Relics of St. Maria Goretti. 2015. https://mariagoretti.com.

Popcak, Gregory K. "'Honey Don'ts' and Helicopters," CatholicCounselors.com. Accessed February 16, 2021 https://Catholiccounselors.com/honey-donts-and-helicopters/.

"Saint Catherine of Siena," Catholicism.org. Accessed February 16, 2021. http://catholicism.org/saint-catherine-of-siena.html.

"Saint Dymphna." Accessed February 16, 2021. https://www.catholic.org/saints/saint.php?saint_id=222.

Sherman, J. Catherine. *Grieving: Inviting God Into My Pain.* iUniverse, 2011.

Spears, Olivia. "Bl. Pier Giorgio Frassati." Catholic Exchange. Accessed February 16, 2021. https://catholicexchange.com/11-reasons-love-bl-pier-giorgio-frassati.

Confraternity of Christian Doctrine. "Matthew." In The New American Bible Revised Edition. Washington: Confraternity of Christian Doctrine, 2010. https://bible.usccb.org/bible/matthew/3.

Wasikowski, John. *Nine Days With Saint Dymphna and Saint Gereban.* John Wasikowski, 2014. Kindle.

ACKNOWLEDGMENTS

A project this heavy cannot happen without many hands reaching out in prayer and support. I offer my immense gratitude to the following:

Sarah Reinhard for reaching out so many times over the years with ideas, enthusiasm, and encouragement.

Mary Beth Baker for welcoming me so warmly into the world of longer-form nonfiction writing.

My fiction tribe: Carolyn Astfalk, Corinna Turner, Theresa Linden, Ellen Gable, Rebecca Martin.

A second thanks to Rebecca Martin for making that leap with me from literature buddy to nonfiction coworkers (but always throwing enough Shakespeare in there to keep us tapped into our roots).

Daniel F. Brown for professional support.

Barb Szyszkiewicz for being a wonderful cheerleader, friend, editor, and for being the Franciscan this Dominican needs.

Margaret Realy for talking me either up or down as needed.

The members of Seeking Mary, Embracing Eve, and my other recovery groups and buddies (you know who you are), for their courage, problem-solving, and example of hope and healing.

My oldest child for keeping me company over coffee on school days.

My middle child for lending me her current edition of the *Catechism*.

My youngest child for keeping Sparkle the Plastic Hawk Decoy by my writing desk.

Scott Cupp for believing in this project and for reaching alongside me for godly healing.

Lastly, thank you to all the composers and musicians who provided me with Marvel movie soundtracks while I wrote. You're the real heroes.

ABOUT THE AUTHOR

Erin McCole Cupp is a wife, mother, and lay Dominican who lives with her family of vertebrates somewhere in the Middle of Nowhere, Pennsylvania. When Erin is not writing, cooking or parenting, she can be found reading, dancing English Country, and dragging loved ones to visitor centers at tourist spots around the country. Get to know Erin, her books, and her joy in sharing God's healing at erinmccolecupp.com.